OBSERVATIONS ON THE ARCHAEOLOGY AND ETHNOLOGY OF NICARAGUA

COLLECTING A VOCABULARY.

OBSERVATIONS ON THE ARCHAEOLOGY
AND ETHNOLOGY OF NICARAGUA

Ephraim G. Squier

With Additional Notes by Frank E. Comparato
Editor

 LABYRINTHOS *1990*

Labyrinthos will appreciate comments on this publication. The publisher will also welcome for consideration proposals for or manuscripts of English translations of other archival materials on pre-Columbian and colonial life in the New World.

TYPOGRAPHICAL NOTE

This edition was partially composed on IBM Magnetic Tape Selectric Composer equipment. In order to present Spanish accents, Press Roman Latin faces have been used. As these fonts lack square brackets, a double virgule (//) is used where brackets are conventionally employed.

Etymological abbreviations: Latin—L.; Mayan—M.; Nahuat, Nahuatl—N.; Spanish—Sp.

Originally published as Ephraim G. Squier, "Observations on the Archaeology and Ethnology of Nicaragua." American Ethnological Society (New York), *Transactions*, Vol. 3 (1853), 83-158.

Additional material copyright (c) 1990 by Labyrinthos

Library of Congress Card Catalog No. 88-82906 / ISBN 0-911437-08-8

Design and Typography by the Editor

Printed in the United States of America

 LABYRINTHOS, 6355 GREEN VALLEY CIRCLE No. 213, CULVER CITY, CALIFORNIA 90230

CONTENTS

ILLUSTRATIONS

INTRODUCTION

If any one supposes that it is an easy task to elicit a satisfactory vocabulary from Indians incapable of comprehending your interest in the matter, and naturally disposed to think that you have a sinister purpose, I commend them //sic// to a trial in Guajiquero //Honduras//! Then there is the other difficulty of making them understand the abstract nature of many of your inquiries, which is so seldom effected that most vocabularies collected by travelers are almost valueless.

Thus: you present your hand, and inquire what it is called. Ten chances to one your Indian will answer by a term signifying *your hand*, or *right hand*, or *your right hand*. Or if you point to your own eye and ask its name, he will most likely answer, *your eye, a blue eye*, or *a black eye*, as the case may be, or *your blue eye*, etc. Point to his eye, and he will reply, *my eye*, or more emphatically, *my own eye*, etc., etc. Unless the interrogator has a quick ear, and adroitly varies his questions so as to get at the elementary word, his vocabulary will be a strange jumble of phrases, of little use in comparative philology.

I had a protracted effort to obtain from my Alcalde the word for woman. It was in vain that I sought to impress the abstract idea of woman on his mind. The colloquy ran something in this wise:

Q.: What do you call a woman in *lengua* //the local native language//?
A.: (after a pause) Sometimes Mary, sometimes Concepción, and sometimes—
Q.: No, not their individual names, but as distinguished from men?
A.: Why, if she is my wife, I call her my wife, and if my sister, I call her my sister.
Q.: That is not what I want. How do you distinguish women from men?
A.: They are dressed differently.
Q.: I mean in speaking of them—in your language?
A.: I have told you; some are called Mary—
Q.: (impatiently) No, no, my friend, a simple woman—woman singly, in herself, as distinct from a man?
A.: Ah! (with sudden animation, and as if gratified with having at last caught my meaning) You mean one who isn't married! She is called *soltera*! (Spanish for old maid). She has no name in *lengua*! . . ./1/

Ephraim G. Squier (1821-1888) was a man of two worlds. He thrust himself into strange and foreign places to relish the delights of challenge and discovery, and he rummaged in libraries and museums to pore over the ancient and modern records of those who went before him. Trained as a journalist, he was ever reporting, ever writing.

Hard on the heels of Stephens and Catherwood, Squier also hoped to discover and record American civilizations long obscured by uncharted jungle, mountain, and savannah. As United States consul to Central America he expected to find himself in the Maya realm—or better, in a region even less known but perhaps more accomplished. Nicaragua, alas, was an archaeological disappointment, but he made the most of his opportunities.

At the same time Squier read all he could find on his exotic destination. Oviedo in 1528 had been one of the first Europeans there, and had recorded some of the most exciting events and observations of all his encounters. His chronicle was not fully published until 1840—and even then not available in English. Squier's quotations and excerpts from Oviedo and others were probably among the first translations into English; his assimilations of Ternaux-Compans' renditions (in French) of Nahuatl and other native languages remain embedded in Squier's copy as reminders of a perilous philological journey to reach fascinated American readers.

Squier quickly perceived he could introduce the Nicaragua in which he was interested with translations from Oviedo and other chroniclers, and also furnish his own descriptions of present-day conditions, which were nearly idyllic (for his interocean canal proposals). But Oviedo had already called Nicaragua pure bliss:/2/

As to fertility of this realm and the situation of the land itself, and its healthful and mild climate, and its excellent waters and fisheries, and its abundance of hunting and game, there is nothing in all of the Indies which, feature for feature, surpasses it //Nicaragua//. . . . Mohammed's Paradise. . . .

Squier promptly forgot Stephens and Catherwood and soon followed Oviedo, Las Casas, and others, quoting them liberally as he went along. He collected vocabularies for the new science of linguistics and he had an artist sketch some curious "alter-ego" statuary for the new Smithsonian Institution—and sent along a few real specimens as well.

Returning from his one-year diplomatic trip in 1850, the prolific "Minister of the United States to the Government of Central America" probably had his book on Nicaragua entirely written by the time his ship reached port.

The work appeared in 1852 (see Bibliography). At the same time to his friends at the American Ethnological Society he must have read large portions of it, which were quickly incorporated into its *Transactions*. The *Transaction* article, in fact, was nothing more than an almost verbatim restatement of portions of the book.

For Nicaragua, such as it was, Squier was indeed the "Stephens" he wanted to be. His collections of Nicaraguan sketches and sculptures became the happy foundation for that reputation. "The man who can truly be called their discoverer," wrote Deuel, "is E. George Squier."/3/ "Squier and Lehmann //director of the Ethnological Institute of the Berlin Ethnographical Museum// give much linguistic and some ethnographic information concerning various tribes of Nicaragua," said William Duncan Strong in 1940, finding at that time that Central American linguistics were so little studied the literature still "verges on the absurd." "Squier makes a few remarks on Lenca ceremonials //sic// some eighty years ago," he added, but data everywhere were fragmentary and disappointing. The situation today is a little better (see Bibliography)./4/

Gonzalo Fernández de Oviedo y Valdéz (1478-1557) came to America 1514 in the expedition of Pedro Arias de Avila (or Pedrarias Dávila), who quickly distinguished himself, in Sauer's words, in "naked greed and cold cruelty." Oviedo became an overseer at the mines and smelters of Arias de Avila's Castilla del Oro, the Colombia-Venezuela coast. He returned to Spain a year later, disgusted by the rapacity and mismanagement of his countrymen. Oviedo nevertheless returned to Darién (Colombia) in 1520 and remained there five years collecting materials for the books he would write.

In 1527 Oviedo went to Nicaragua where, for about two years, he traveled and recorded his recollections. When Arias de Avila became governor there, Oviedo was in some personal danger and he again returned to Spain. Like Las Casas, he was gradually able to impress upon the Crown the magnitude of these Spanish excesses.

In 1552 Oviedo was named official chronicler of the Indies and retired to Hispaniola until his death. His *Historia general y natural de las Indias*—published 1535 (21 volumes), with some additional parts in 1547 and 1851-55—despite considerable ethnographic coverage, depicts the Indians with some derision and impatience. His observations nevertheless have enormous interest and importance.

After the first Spaniards in Nicaragua had reported baptizing thousands of natives, Arias de Avila perversely sought to discredit their efforts; he commissioned a relative, Fray Francisco Bobadilla (not to be confused with the governor of that name), to determine just how successful the earlier "conversions" to Christianity had been. Bobadilla's quaint methods and results, dutifully recorded by Oviedo, appear here.

For Bobadilla the Indians described their arrival in Nicaragua (and other migrations), marriage and burial practices, calendar, gods, confession, and many other customs—"overall," said Abel-Vidor, "this is an astonishing array of ethnographic information, even if collected in the context of a formal interview. . . ."/5/ Oviedo might have had even more to report; he later explained:/6/

> More ceremonies and rites and customs and notable things remain to be told that have not been told of this province //Nicaragua// and its territories, and to recount them all would be impossible, as much because it is difficult to be certain of details for the diversity of languages, as because war and contact with Christians and the passage of time have consumed and put an end to the lives of the old people and even the young, and because of the greed of the judges, governors, and others who were in such haste to remove Indians from their land as slaves. . . .

To Squier's regret, Nicaragua boasted no Copán or Chichén Itzá, but it did have some truly amazing—living—communities: people who spoke Nahuatl-related languages, the language of the Mexican Aztecs dwelling some 1500 miles to the north. How this came to the attention of the Spaniards, and how it came to be explained by a variety of commentators since Oviedo, are recounted here.

1. E. G. Squier, "A Visit to the Guajiquero Indians." *Harpers' New Monthly*, October 1859, 615. Squier's one-day visit to the Guajiquero Indians was the only nineteenth-century account of these people, and Bancroft used his description of a dance he saw there. The Guajiqueros were probably a Lenca tribe. (Stansifer, 178.)

2. Healy, 10.

3. Deuel, 155-56. Deuel reproduced in full Squier's popular description of the statuary: "Ancient Monuments in the Islands of Lake Nicaragua, Central America." *Literary World*, 16 March 1850, 269-70, 304-5.

4. Strong, 383.

5. Abel-Vidor, 263, 267-68, 285; Keen, 79; Sauer, xii, 248; Squier, i 192.

6. Abel-Vidor, 285.

OBSERVATIONS ON THE ARCHAEOLOGY AND ETHNOLOGY OF NICARAGUA

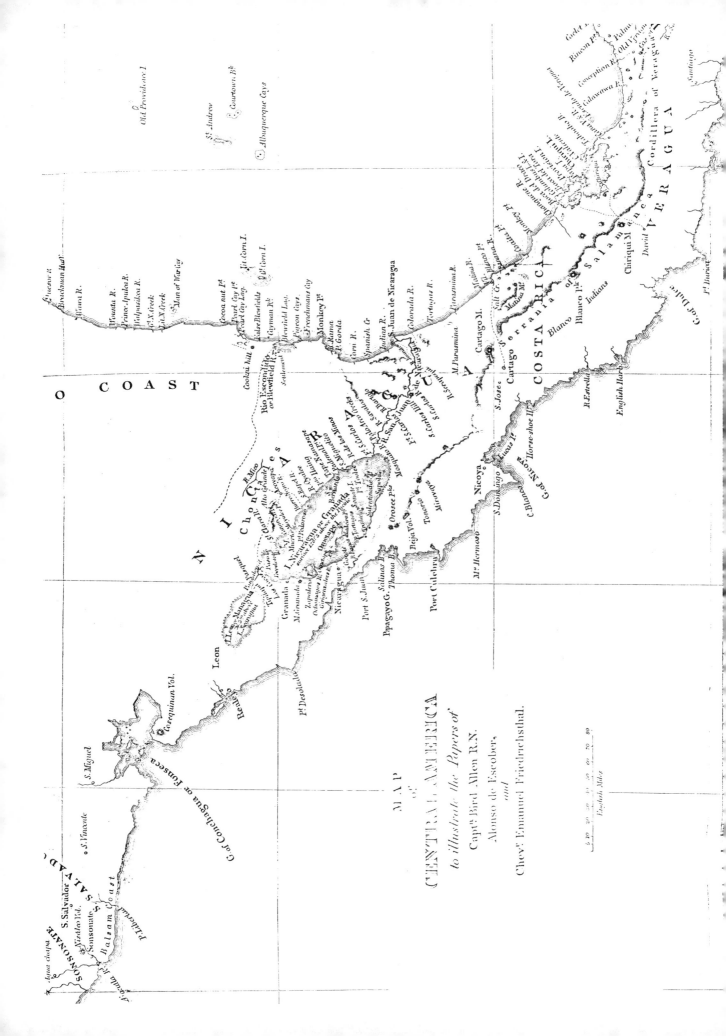

MAP
of
CENTRAL AMERICA
to illustrate the Papers of
Captn. Bird Allen R.N.
Alonso de Escobar,
and
Chevr. Emanuel Friedrichsthal.

5 10 20 30 40 50 60 70 80
English Miles

OBSERVATIONS ON THE ARCHAEOLOGY AND ETHNOLOGY OF NICARAGUA

PRESENT CONDITION OF THE INDIANS OF NICARAGUA

The aborigines of Nicaragua, as also of the other States of Central America, still constitute numerically the predominating portion of the population; and if we include the people of other races amalgamated with them they undoubtedly comprehend three-fourths of the entire inhabitants.

Most of these are what may be called civilized; but there are many tribes occupying large tracts of unexplored country, generally denominated "Indios Bravos,"/1/ who are more or less savage and whose numbers we have no means of estimating. They undoubtedly retain their primitive habits, very little modified from what they were before the period of the Discovery. But among the civilized Indians of Nicaragua, although mingling freely with the inhabitants of European descent, there has not been that change from their original habits which might at first be supposed. Indeed, it is, in many respects, hard to say whether the conquerors have assimilated most to the Indians, or the Indians most to the Spaniards.

The Indians of today occupy the towns that their ancestors occupied; and the departmental and other subdivisions of the country coincide very nearly with the ancient principalities or chieftaincies. The prefects, or heads of these departments, have only supplanted the *caziques*;/2/ and the existing municipalities only supply the places of the *guegues*, or councils of old men. Many of the social, as well as civil institutions of the country, have been recognized and perpetuated by the Spaniards; and some of the ceremonies of the aboriginal ritual have also been incorporated among the rites of the Catholic Church. For, however rude and subverting the first shock of Spanish conquest in America, the subsequent policy of Spain, framed and directed by the famous Council of the Indies,/3/ was that of conciliation. In common with the Church it conceded much to the habits and feelings of the aborigines, and to a certain extent conformed to them.

Thus much may be said of the Indians of Central America generally; but the following observations must be understood to refer specifically to those of Nicaragua, although perhaps quite true of those of the other States. In character they are singularly docile and industrious, and constitute what would, in some countries, be called an excellent "rural population." They are a smaller race of men than the Indians of the United States, but have fine muscular developments, and a singularly mild and soft expression of countenance. In color also they are lighter, and their features less strongly marked. Some of the women are exceedingly pretty, and when young have figures beautifully and classically moulded. They are entirely unobtrusive in their manners, seldom speaking unless first addressed, and are always kind and hospitable to strangers. They are not warlike, but brave; and when reduced to the necessity, fight with desperate obstinacy.

The agriculture of the state is almost entirely carried on by them; but they are not deficient in mechanical skill, and with the rudest tools often produce the most delicate and elaborate articles of workmanship. The women manufacture a large quantity of cotton for their own consumption and for sale. And in riding through the Indian towns in the afternoon no spectacle is more common than to see women naked to the waist, seated in the doorway of almost every hut, or beneath the shadow of an adjacent tree, busily engaged in spinning cotton.

A little foot-wheel, such as was formerly in use for spinning flax in our own country, is here commonly used for this purpose. But the aboriginal contrivance is not yet wholly replaced. It is simple, consisting of a thin spindle of wood fifteen or sixteen inches in length, which is passed through a fly, or wheel, of hard, heavy wood, six inches in diameter,

1. Sp. *bravo*, brave, manful, savage, wild; also rude, unpolished, uncivilized.
2. The *cazique* (or *cacique*, an Arawak word) was a hereditary ruler sometimes equal to a king; lesser caziques were chiefs of districts or clans. For *guegues* (below), see n. 86 and text following.
3. The Royal Council of the Indies in Seville was formed 1524 for the political administration of America; see n. 26.

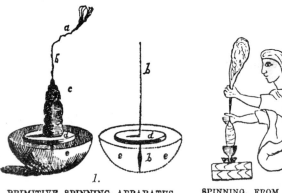

PRIMITIVE SPINNING APPARATUS.

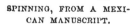
SPINNING, FROM A MEXI-
CAN MANUSCRIPT.

3. WEAVING, FROM A MEXICAN MANUSCRIPT.

resembling the wheel of a pulley, except that it is convex instead of concave on the edge. The spindle thus resembles a gigantic top. When used, it is placed in a calabash,/4/ or hollowed piece of wood, to prevent it from toppling over when not in motion. A thread is attached to it just above the fly, and it is then twirled rapidly between the thumb and forefinger. The momentum of the fly keeps it in motion for half a minute, and meantime the thread is drawn out by the hands of the operator, from the pile of prepared cotton which she holds in her lap. It is then wound on the spindle, and the process repeated, until the spindle is full of thread.

In Figure 1, *a* represents the cotton; *b, b*, the spindle; *d*, the fly; *c*, the thread already spun and wound; and *e, e*, the outlines of the calabash. A precisely similar mode of spinning was practiced by the ancient Mexicans, who, however, inserted the lower end of the spindle in a hole made in a block of wood, as shown in Figure 2. The mode of weaving among the Indians of Nicaragua was anciently the same as that of the Mexicans, which is sufficiently well illustrated in Figure 3, copied from the Codex Mendoza,/5/ a Mexican manuscript or painting.

Some of the cotton fabrics manufactured by the Indians are very durable, and woven in tasteful figures of various colors. The color most valued is the Tyrian purple, obtained from the murex shell-fish,/6/ which is found upon the Pacific coast of Nicaragua. This color is produced of any desirable depth and tone, and is permanent; unaffected alike by exposure to the sun and to the action of alkali.

The process of dyeing the thread illustrates the patient assiduity of the Indians. It is taken to the sea-side, when a sufficient number of shells are collected; and these being dried from the sea water, the work is commenced. Each shell is taken up singly; and a slight pressure upon the valve which closes its mouth forces out a few drops of the coloring fluid, which is then almost destitute of color. In this each thread is dipped singly, and, after absorbing enough of the precious liquid, is carefully drawn out between the thumb and finger, and laid aside to dry. Whole days and nights are spent in this tedious process, until the work is completed. At first the thread is of a dull blue color; but upon exposure to the atmosphere it acquires the desired tint. The fish is not destroyed by the operation, but is returned to the sea, when it lays in a new stock of coloring matter for a future occasion.

The manufacture of "*petates*,"/7/ or variegated mats, from the bark of the palm, and hammocks from the "*pita*," a species of agave, is exclusively in Indian hands. They are also skilfull in the manufacture of pottery, which has remained unchanged from the period before the Conquest. The "*cantaros*," water-jars, and other vessels in common use among all classes, are made by them. They are formed by hand without the aid of the potter's wheel, and are variously and often elaborately colored and ornamented, baked, and are, when intended for purposes requiring it, partially glazed.* The

4. See n. 9.

5. The Codex (or "Colección") Mendoza, a book of royal succession and tribute, is apparently a colonial-age copy of a precolumbian original. The illustrations Squier identifies as "from a Mexican Manuscript" and the animal heads in the calendar tables at the end are from the Mendoza.

6. The murex or Muricidae family of mollusks yields a purple dye. Two other species, Purpura and *Thais kiosquiformi*, were similarly exploited in Guatemala. (Squier, ii 45.)

7. For petate see n. 98; for pita, n. 133.

*Mr. W. H. Edwards, in his narrative, *A Voyage up the Amazon* //. . . including a Residence at Pará*. London: Murray, 1847, p. 89—a subsequent edition// p. 114, describes the preparation and painting of pottery by the Indians on

water jars, however, are porous, so as to admit of enough water passing through to keep the outer surface covered with moisture, the evaporation of which rapidly and effectually cools the contents of the vessel. Oviedo/8/ commends highly the skill which the ancient inhabitants displayed in the manufacture of their pottery, and which is very well sustained, both by the fragments which are found and by the wares which the Indians still manufacture. "They make basins, plates, jars, and pitchers of very fine pottery, black and smooth as velvet, and brilliant as jet. I have brought some specimens, which are so fine that they might be offered to a prince."

They also make drinking vessels from the calabash;/9/ the largest varieties are called "*guacals*," or "*aguacals*," and the smaller ones, made from the long or pear-shaped calabash, "*jicaras*." These last are often tastefully carved upon their exteriors and are generally used instead of tumblers. It is indispensable that "*tiste*"/10/ should be served in jicarras; and among the people at large they are also used for coffee and chocolate. But as their bottoms are round, little carved stands are made to receive them. The Indians near the city of Nicaragua make similar cups from a variety of the coconut peculiar to that vicinity, which are celebrated throughout the country for their beauty of shape and ornament. They are black and highly polished, and, when mounted with silver, are greatly prized by foreigners.

The dress of the Indians is exceedingly simple. On ordinary occasions the women wear only a white or flowered skirt, fastened around the waist, leaving the upper part of the person entirely exposed or but partially covered by a handkerchief fastened around the neck. In Masaya/11/ and some other places a square piece of cloth of native manufacture—and of precisely the same style and pattern with that used for the same purpose before the Discovery—supplies the place of the skirt. It is fastened in some incomprehensible way, without the aid of strings or pins, and falls from the hips a little below the knees. The *guipil*/12/ and *nagua* are, however, adopted in nearly all the large towns and are everywhere worn on festival days and Sundays.

The men wear a kind of cotton drawers, fastened above the hips, but frequently reaching no lower than the knees. Sandals supply the place of shoes, but for the most part, both sexes go with their feet bare. The taste for ornament is universal; and a rosary, to which is attached a little golden, silver, or ebony cross, is suspended from the necks of male and female, old and young. They are also fond of flowers, and the girls are seldom without some of them entwined among the luxuriant locks of their long black hair or braided in a chaplet, and encircling their foreheads.

The Indian *pueblos*,/13/ in common with the *barrios* of some of the towns, hold lands in their corporate capacity.

that river. The brushes or pencils were the small species of palms, and the coloring matter the simplest kinds. The blue was indigo; black, the juice of the mandioca //tapioca//; green, the juice of some other plant; and the red and yellow, clays. The colors were applied in squares and circles, or if anything imitative was intended, in the rudest outlines. The *glazing* was produced by a resinous gum found in the forests, which was gently rubbed over the vessels, previously warmed over a bed of coals. This description applies equally to the modes practiced in Nicaragua.

//Both asterisked notes and those in parentheses are the author's. This footnote originally appeared in the text of Squier's *Nicaragua* (n. 72), essentially Edwards' words verbatim. (Squier, i 288.)

8. See n. 78.

9. From the *Relación* of Mérida: "There are also some trees called *luch* //Crescentia cujete L.//, which means trees of vessels, which produce a fruit of the size of a bowling ball. . . . This fruit is green and has a rind as thick . . . as a *real*, very hard, and the interior is like that of a melon although it is not good to eat. The Indians divide this fruit into halves, and by removing the inside, without any further work they are made into vessels which the Indians use for drinking which we Spaniards call *jícarras*, which is a Mexican word." (Landa, 90.)

10. Today, tiste is a drink made of toasted maize flour, cacao, arnotto, and sugar.

11. Near Masaya Volcano; see n. 28.

12. The *güipil* or *huipil* (N. *huipilli*) was a woman's blouse, put on over the head. In Mexico it was worn by the middle and upper classes. The (Haitian) *nagua* or (Sp.) *enagua* was a short skirt or underskirt. (Soustelle, 134-35; Durán, 103, 250.)

13. *Pueblo* refers to an Indian community gathered, usually by the religious, to facilitate the teaching of Christianity. The *barrio* is a "quarter" or section of a town or pueblo, usually with its own officials.

JICARA. GUACAL. CONTRARO. TINAJA.

These lands are inalienable and are leased to the inhabitants at low and almost nominal rates. Every citizen is entitled to a sufficient quantity to enable him to support himself and his family; for which he pays from four *reales*/14/ (half a dollar) to two dollars a year. This practice seems to have been of aboriginal institution; for under the ancient Indian organization, the *right to live* was recognized as a fundamental principle in the civil and social organization. No man was supposed to be entitled to more land than was necessary to his support; nor was he permitted to hold more than that, to the exclusion or injury of others.

The conquest of Nicaragua was effected with no less violence than that of Mexico and Peru; and if we may credit the account of Las Casas,/15/ the pious bishop of Chiapa, who visited the country in person, it was both attended and followed by extraordinary cruelties. He charges the enormity chiefly upon Pedro Arias de Avila,/16/ Governor of Darién, who sent Córdova to subdue the country and who himself afterwards became its governor.

The Indians of this province //Las Casas says// were naturally of a mild and peaceable temper; yet, notwithstanding this, the Governor—or rather, Tyrant—with the ministers of his cruelty, treated them in the same manner as they did those of the other kingdoms. They committed murders and robberies—more than it is possible for pen to relate. Upon the slightest pretexts the soldiers massacred the inhabitants without regard to age, sex, or condition. They exacted from them certain measures of corn, and certain numbers of slaves, and, if these were not rendered, hesitated not to kill the delinquents. And the country being a plain, the people were unable to escape to the mountains as they did elsewhere, and were consequently at the mercy of the Spanish horse. They carried off many thousands as slaves, slaying those who fainted or wearied on the march.

The Governor once arbitrarily changed the distribution of the Indians, conveying most of them to his favorites, to the exclusion of those with whom he was displeased. The result of this was a great scarcity of food; and the Spaniards, seizing upon the provisions of the Indians, caused a great distress and induced a disorder which destroyed upwards of thirty thousand of the people.

All the cities and fields around them were like pleasant gardens, which the Spaniards cultivated according to the share which each one had assigned to him by lot; and to save their own revenues they supported themselves from the stores of the Indians, thus consuming, in a short time, what these poor people had got together with great care and toil. Nobles, women, and children were all compelled to work day and night; many died under the burdens which were imposed upon them. For they obliged them to carry on their shoulders to the ports, which were in some cases distant thirty leagues,/17/ the planks and timbers used in building vessels.

Las Casas, however, regards the practice of exacting slaves from the caziques, for transportation and sale elsewhere, as one of the chief causes of the depopulation of the country. Five or six shiploads were annually taken to Peru and Panama, and sold there. He calculates that half a million of Indians were thus drawn out of Nicaragua alone; but this number appears incredible. The statement that from fifty to sixty thousand perished in the wars of the Conquest is, perhaps, nearer the truth.

But whatever their former condition, the Indians of Nicaragua no longer labor under any disabilities. They enjoy equal privileges with the whites and may aspire to any position, however high, both in the Church and State. The system of *peonage* (slavery under a less repugnant name) is here unknown. Yet the Indian retains his traditionary

14. With 8 reales ("pieces of eight") to the peso, Squier here gives the value of the peso as equal to 1 U.S. dollar.

15. Fray Bartolomé de Las Casas (1474-1566), a Dominican, was called "Apostle of the Indies," long preaching and writing against Indian abuses. In Verapaz he peacefully won over the fierce natives after Spanish soldiers had thrice failed. He was bishop of Chiapa (Chiapas) 1544-47. (Squier, i 291.)

16. Pedro Arias d'Avila (or Pedrarias Dávila, 1440?-1531), Spanish soldier, was governor of Darién, or Panama, 1514-26. He went to Nicaragua in 1526 and established an extremely profitable slave trade which took 400,000 natives from that country alone. Extremely cruel, according to Oviedo he killed 2 million Indians. Francisco Fernández Córdoba (1475?-1526) in 1514 accompanied Pedrarias to Panama; the latter in 1522 sent him to take possession of Nicaragua. He founded Granada and León (1523), declaring himself independent, but he was surprised by Pedrarias and executed. (HMAI, xiii; León-Portilla, 19; Las Casas, 178-82; Sauer, 248; Radell, 63, 66, 68.)

17. The Spanish league was variously 2½ to 3½ miles in length.

deference for the white man, and tacitly admits his superiority. In some of the States of Central America a jealousy of caste has been artfully excited by unscrupulous partisans for unworthy purposes, which has led to most deplorable results; but in Nicaragua if this feeling exists at all it is only in a latent form. At any rate, it has never displayed itself in any of those frightful demonstrations which have almost desolated Guatemala and portions of Peru, and which threaten the entire extinction of the white race in Yucatan. This quiet, however, may be that of the slumbering volcano; and its continuance may depend very much upon the judicious encouragement of white emigration from the United States and from Europe./18/

GEOGRAPHICAL DISTRIBUTION

Such, in brief, is the present condition of the Indians of Nicaragua; but the objects of science can only be promoted by the presentation of such facts as shall serve to fix their ethnical position in respect to the other great aboriginal families of the continent. My personal observations, directed to this end, were almost wholly confined to the region around the great lakes of the interior; a region unerringly marked out, by the circumstances of geographical position and physical conformation, as the theater of vaster enterprises than human daring has hitherto conceived or human energy yet attempted.

Here nature has lavished her richest gifts and assumed her most magnificent forms: high volcanoes, gentle slopes, level plains, and broad and beautiful lakes and rivers, are here combined with a fertility of soil and a salubriousness of climate probably unsurpassed by any equal extent of country under the tropics. These were conditions eminently favorable for bringing together primitive communities of men and for nurturing and sustaining a vast population. That it did so we have the testimony of all the early chroniclers; and he who has passed over its broad plains and luxuriant slopes and observed its attractions and resources will be prepared to credit the assertion of the pious Las Casas that it was "one of the best-peopled countries in all America."

From the testimony of the early explorers, from the monuments and other existing sources of information, we know that the Indians of Nicaragua were then, as now, divided into two widely separated if not radically distinct families, corresponding very nearly with the natural divisions of the country.

Upon the low alluvions, and among the dense, dank forests of the Atlantic coast, there existed a few scanty wandering tribes, maintaining a precarious subsistence by hunting and fishing, with little or no agriculture, destitute of civil organizations, with a debased religion, and generally corresponding with the Caribs of the islands, to whom they sustained close affinities. Of these rude tribes it is not my present purpose to speak. A portion of their descendants, still further debased by the introduction of Negro blood, may yet be found in the wretched Moscos/19/ or Mosquitos, who—by a brazen fraud—are attempted to be passed off upon the world as a sovereign nation, comprehending the duties and capable of fulfilling the requirements of government! The few and scattered Melchoras/20/ on the river San Juan are certainly of Carib stock; and it is more than probable that the same is true of the Woolwas,/21/ Ramas, Toacas, and Poyas, and also of the other tribes on the Atlantic coast further to the southward, toward Chiriquí Lagoon, and collectively denominated Bravos.

In the more elevated and salubrious regions around the great lakes of the interior, and upon the slopes of the Pacific, on the other hand, the natives had many features in common with the semi-civilized nations of Mexico, Guatemala, and

18. In the Yucatecan Maya revolt of 1847 the Indians' hatred of both local Spaniards and soldiers from Mexico produced a war lingering until about 1855. The violence was apparently vivid for Squier.

19. Strong (a century later) agreed that the Moscos or Mosquitos were "pitiable" in appearance, especially in contrast to the "splendid" Black Caribs (the "Negro blood" to which Squier refers) of common origin. Their language is almost certainly a form of Chibchan. Squier's "brazen fraud" was a British attempt to establish an "independent" government on the Mosquito shore to strengthen its hold on Belize. (Strong, 380.)

20. The Melchoras apparently spoke a form of Chibchan or Chibcha, the native language of Colombia and Ecuador, spoken by their neighbors in Nicaragua, the Rama. The San Juan River is the border between Nicaragua and Costa Rica. (Kidder, 443.)

21. Squier later identifies the Woolwa (Ulúa, Ulba, Gaula—first encountered on Honduras' Ulúa River) as a tribe

Yucatan, and had made many advances in the same direction with them. Like these, they were divided into numerous tribes or small sovereignties, with separate and independent chiefs or councils of government. With the single exception of those inhabiting the narrow strip of land between Lake Nicaragua and the Pacific,/22/ and who had also spread to the principal islands of the lake, they appear to have been essentially one people, with like habits and customs, a common religion, and speaking—if not the same language—probably dialects of the same language.

The exception to which I here refer is one of the most remarkable facts in the history of the American aborigines. The inhabitants of this narrow isthmus, between the lake and ocean, were Mexicans, speaking the ancient Mexican language and having a civil and social organization, as also a system of religion, identical with those which prevailed among the Aztecs and their affiliated nations. The evidence upon this point, furnished by my own investigations in the country, is conclusive, and will shortly appear. It is only necessary here to say that this fact is sustained by the positive testimony of the historian Oviedo, who was in the country in the years immediately succeeding the Conquest, and who speaks from his own personal knowledge. His language is as follows: "The Niquirans," i.e. the inhabitants of the district between the lake and ocean, "who speak the Mexican language, have the same manners and appearance as the people of New Spain."/23/

The remaining inhabitants of Nicaragua this authority divides into two stocks, viz., those speaking the Choro-tegan/24/ language and its dialects, and the Chontals/25/ or Condals. The first of these, or the Chorotegans, occupied the entire country north of the Niquirans, extending along the Pacific Ocean, between it and Lake Managua, to the borders, and probably for a distance along the shores of the Gulf of Fonseca./26/ They also occupied the country south of the Niquirans and around the Gulf of Nicoya, then called Orotiña. These were again separated into several divisions, all speaking the Chorotegan language or dialects of it:

situated between the western peoples of Nicaragua and the more primitive eastern tribes. The Chibchan-speaking Ramas occupy the Bluefields area (n. 40). Mason listed Squier's "Toacas" as Tawahka, a Suman language (i.e. spoken by the Sumo Indians) but said nothing about it; Kidder called it Chibchan too. Squier's "Poyas" are the Paya, in whom Spinden found South American characteristics; Stone judged them a very simple people in Honduras, also possibly Chibchan. (Doris Stone, "The Ulua Valley and Lake Yojoa." Hay et al., 390; Strong, 383; Lothrop 1940, 426; Kidder, 443; Mason, 73, 86; Palacio, 35.)

22. The narrow strip or isthmus, called Rivas, furnished Healy a variety of Maya and Mexican ceramics whose motifs suggested an arrival date for the Chorotegans (n. 24) of 800-1200 A.D. Foreign pottery continued to arrive until the sixteenth century, some of it "quite Mexicanized designs, including representations of postclassic Mexican deities." These importations were probably introduced by the Nicaráos (n. 23). Lake Nicaragua, about 100 miles long, contains the islands of Ometepe (n. 39) and Zapatero (n. 74). (Healy, 345.)

23. Squier's "Niquirans" in Spanish are the Nicaráos, a people originally migrating from the Cholulá area of Mexico (n. 120). They dated their departure for Nicaragua from the fall of Tula (n. 66), bringing with them cacao cultivation (which they monopolized), human sacrifice, the calendar, and a pantheon of gods. When they arrived they dispossessed the earlier Chiapanecan tribes on the isthmus of Rivas (naming them "Chorotegans"—n. 24). Much of this history was communicated to the Spaniards by a chief named Nicaráo who, according to Peter Mártyr, was "born near the //native// kingdom of Nicaragua and, educated //in Spanish//, spoke fluently in the language of both." See also n. 105. (Radell, 46; Stone, 218; León-Portilla, 13, 19, 26-27, 96, 99; Healy, 7; Spinden, 544-45.)

24. The "Chorotegan culture area," according to Spinden, included parts of Nicaragua, Honduras, and Costa Rica and extended all the way to Panama. It was probably a major source of precious metals for the Mexicans, suggesting that their arrival at Rivas was not entirely accidental. In both Niquiran and Chorotegan communities the development of commercial—long-distance—marketing was important. The Chorotegans nevertheless had no writing system. (Herbert J. Spinden, "Diffusion of Maya Astronomy." Hay et al., 164; Spinden, 529, 544; Healy, 2, 290; Davies, 119; Lehmann, 1011.)

25. The Chontal (Chondal, Condal) Indians in Nicaragua were especially primitive and cannibalistic; they were called "dumb animals" by other tribes.

26. The Gulf of Fonseca was named for Juan Rodríguez de Fonseca (1451-1524), chaplain to Isabella and Ferdinand; he soon opposed both Columbus and Cortés and formed the Council of the Indies. The Gulf of Nicoya was earlier called Gulf of Orotiña (n. 30) and Nicaragua. (Lehmann, 1002.)

27. Mason listed Diria and Nagrandan (below) as extinct varieties of Mangue, an Otomanguean (Chorotegan)

I. *The Dirians*,/27/ or "people of the hills," who occupied the territory lying between the upper extremity of Lake Nicaragua, the river Tipitapa, and the southern half of Lake Managua and the Pacific, whose principal towns were situated where now stand the cities of Granada (then called Salteba),/28/ Masaya, and Managua, and the villages of Tipitapa, Diriomo, and Diriamba. According to Oviedo they were true Chorotegans.

II. *The Nagrandans*, or people of Nagrando, those speaking the Nagrandan dialect. They occupied what is now called the Plain of León, or the district between the northern extremity of Lake Managua and the Pacific. The name is preserved in that of the City of León, which is still sometimes called León de Nagrando.

III. *The Cholutecans*,/29/ speaking the Cholutecan dialect, situated to the northward of the Nagrandans, and extending along the Gulf of Fonseca, into what is now the territory of Honduras. A town and river in the territory here indicated still bear the name of Choluteca which, however, is a Mexican name.

IV. *The Orotiñans*,/30/ occupying the country around the Gulf of Nicoya and to the southward of Lake Nicaragua.

Concerning the Indians of the Chorotegan stock, Oviedo observes that they were the enemies of the Niquirans and that "their languages, manners, customs, and ceremonies were so different" as to be utterly incomprehensible to the other. He nevertheless adds that their religion was the same; and here it may be observed that all the religions of the semi-civilized nations of the central parts of the continent approximated to a common type.

The Chondals or Chontals, the third great division mentioned by Oviedo, occupied the wide, mountainous region, still bearing the name of Chontales, situated to the northward of Lake Nicaragua and midway between the nations already named and the savage hordes bordering the Caribbean Sea, with whom, it is possible, they may have in some degree assimilated. "These Indians," says Oviedo, "have no connection with the Chorotegans and Niquirans, and speak a language as different from theirs as the Basque is from the German." He nevertheless leaves the inference that their religion was very much the same. Herrera/31/ adds that they were "a mountainous people and clownish"; and I am informed by the Abbé Brasseur de Bourbourg/32/ that the name itself, in one of the Maya dialects, signifies "strangers," or people from abroad.

The chroniclers seem to agree in representing the Chorotegans as the original occupants and predominating family in the country, the *autochthones*. "Those speaking the Chorotegan language," said Oviedo, "are the aborigines of the country, and its ancient masters." Herrera asserts that among them those speaking the Cholutecan language were "the original and most ancient, held the estates, and had the cacao-nuts, which were the money and wealth of the country." It is difficult to understand what is meant by this observation, unless it is that there existed among the people a class arrogating, like the Incas, a superiority over the others and speaking a "court language," or one in some respects differing from theirs.

It seems, therefore, that at the time of the Discovery there existed in Nicaragua two grand families of Indians, whose probable relations and subdivisions are exhibited in the following table:

language. (Mason, 80.)

28. Salteba (Nicaráo, *xalteba, xalteua,* "sand and stone") today is a barrio of Granada. Masaya Volcano is noteworthy. In a 1612 relación (quoted in Landa) Tomás Lopéz Medel described its ritual use:

> In time of great necessity they sacrificed many children in that volcano of Masaya: ... Those who were to be sacrificed were presented to the priest and they all went in procession to that volcano and took the children whom they were going to cast into it. And when they had arrived and performed certain ceremonies the priest took each one of them separately and threw them into the terrible fire where they would be consumed and destroyed before reaching it. And this was the most famous sacrifice. ...

Both Oviedo and Bobadilla climbed to the top, and Oviedo mentioned "many fables" about it; see also n. 75. Tipitapa (below), according to Oviedo, was the name of a cazique. (Lehmann, 1014; Squier, i 218, 221; ii 123-24, 194; Landa, 224; O&V.)

29. See nn. 24, 62.

30. Squier discarded the tilde for both Orotiña and Orotiñans, the latter as speakers of Orotiña, a language in the Chorotegan family. (Mason, 80.)

31. See n. 80.

32. Charles Brasseur de Bourbourg (1814-74), as a French missionary and historian in Mexico and Central America found and published many original manuscripts and codices.

I. SEMI-CIVILIZED		II. SAVAGE	
CHOROTEGANS {	*Dirians* *Nagrandans* *Orotiñans*	CARIBS {	Embracing the Waiknas, or Moscos, Melchoras, Woolwas, Toacas, Poyas, and the other detached tribes situated on the Caribbean Sea, and to the east and southward of the Gulf of Nicoya.
CHOLUTECANS	A Mexican colony		
NIQUIRANS	A Mexican colony		
CHONDALS {	Approximating to the savage tribes		

Oviedo informs us that there were five totally distinct languages spoken in Nicaragua, and Gómera/33/ enumerates them as follows, viz., the Niquiran or Mexican, the Chorotegan, Orotiñan, Chondal, and Carabisi or Carib. The general geographical distribution of these languages will be inferred from what has already been said of the distribution of the various aboriginal stocks in Nicaragua. The Chondal, according to Hervás,/34/ extended as far as Oaxaca. This could not have been the fact unless it was identical with—or closely related to—the Maya Quiché,/35/ Poconchí, and Huasteca, which hardly harmonizes with the concurrent testimony of the chroniclers that the Chondals were an exceedingly rough people, speaking a rude language.

LANGUAGES

Previous to my visit to Nicaragua no vocabularies of any of these languages were in existence. From the Indians of Subtiaba,/36/ near León, in the north-western part of the country, I procured a vocabulary of about two hundred words; and another vocabulary of about the same number of words, from the Indians of Masaya, a hundred miles to the southward of León, and in the territory immediately adjoining that, which we know was occupied by the Niquirans, or the Mexican colony. These two languages have no verbal resemblances, whatever similarity may have existed in their grammatical features; and as Oviedo, in one or two places, says expressly that the Indians around the Lake of Masaya spoke the Chorotegan language, we are driven to the conclusion that what was spoken near León was the Orotiñan. This was undoubtedly spoken by the Indians south of the Niquirans, around the Gulf of Orotiña, where the volcano of Oroti or Orosi still perpetuates their name.

But until we have vocabularies from the known seats of the Orotiñans I shall not venture to call the language which was spoken on the Plain of León by that name. Meantime, I prefer to call it, from the aboriginal name of that district, *Nagrandan.* The language of which I procured a vocabulary at Masaya, following the authority of Oviedo, I have called Chorotegan, or Dirian. Oviedo gives but one word of this language, viz., *nambi*, dog,/37/ which is the precise word still retained. Some of the names of places and natural objects within the area in which this language was spoken seem to have a relationship to certain Peruvian names. Thus Momobacho, Momotombo, and others, sound wonderfully like Moyobamba, Tambobamba, Guamabacho, etc. It would be interesting to take up the suggestion and inquire whether

33. Francisco López de Gómera (1510-1560?), Cortés' chaplain in Spain, wrote a highly lauditory biography of the conquistador, not always accurate in some matters.

34. Lorenzo Hervás y Panduro (1735-1809), a Spanish priest and philologist, spent some time in America and later was a librarian in Rome. Among his many works are some early examples of scientific anthropology.

35. The Quiché and the Cakchiquel, both of highland Guatemala, traced their origin to Tula (n. 66); they subdued the native Mam (n. 55) and Pokomam. The highland Pokonchí language is also closely allied to Pokomam, a "Quichoid" language. The Huasteca or Huaxteca occupied the Veracruz area of Mexico, their "Mayoid" language similar to Chontal (n. 25). (Mason, 71, 107-108.)

36. Subtiaba, an Indian community, was originally chosen for the site of León. Assigned here for 3 months, Bobadilla (n. 109) charged 40 beans per baptism (its population was over 100,000). "One million six hundred thousand grains of cacao," Squier marveled. "Pious Bobadilla!" But when a bishop was killed here in 1549 the Pope reportedly cursed the place—and a series of disasters followed. In 1610 León was moved to its present location at the foot of Momotombo (n. 74). (Strong, 384; Squier, i 257, 324, 326.)

37. See two tables in "Language" section, and n. 139.

there is really any relationship between the languages of Peru and Central America; but this I have not now the means of doing./38/

From the Indians yet residing on the Island of Ometepec/39/ I procured with great difficulty a few words and some of their numerals. This island was occupied by the Niquirans, and the words which I recovered coincide precisely with the Mexican. Indeed, the very name of this island, distinguished for two high volcanic peaks, is pure Mexican, *ome*, two, and *tepec*, mountain.

The region of Chontales was visited by my friend Mr. Julius Froebel/40/ in the summer of this year (1851). He penetrated to the head waters of the Río Mico, Escondido, or Bluefields, where he found the Indians to be agriculturists, partially civilized, and generally speaking the Spanish language. They are called Caribs/41/ by their Spanish neighbors, but have themselves a vague tradition that they came originally from the shores of Lake Managua. Mr. Froebel procured a brief vocabulary of their original language which, however, seems to have little affinity to any of the languages spoken in other parts of the country, on the coast, or in the interior. I have elsewhere given it the name of Chondal,/42/ from the fact that it exists in the district of Chontales, and to distinguish it from the others. But I have since ascertained that it is the true language of a tribe called the Woolwas, lying intermediately between the remnants of semi-civilized stocks and the savage Moscans or Waiknas on the coast.

The following brief table comprises words from the various languages ascertained to have existed in Nicaragua. A few words of Mexican have been introduced to facilitate comparison with the Niquiran, which, however, is really Mexican, differing from the latter in no essential respect, except that the terminals *tl* or *tli* are contracted or wholly omitted:

COMPARATIVE TABLE

English	Nagrandan	Chorotegan or Dirian	Niquiran	Mexican	Waikna or Moscan	Woolwa
God	—	gopaseme	teot	teotl	—	—
Man	rahpa	nuho	tlacat	tlacatl	waikna	all
Woman	rapaku	naseyomo	ciuat	ciuatl	mairen	yall
Head	a'cu	goochemo	tzonteco	totzontecon	lel	tunni
Foot	naku	graho	hixt	icxitl	mena	calni
Dog	romao	nambi	izcuindi	itzcuintli	yul	sulo
Deer	—	numbongame	mazat	mazatl	sula	—
Rabbit	—	—	toste	tochtli	kaia	—
Fire	ahku	nahu	tlet	tletl	panta	cuh
Water	eeia	nimbu	at	atl	lia	wass?
House	guah	nahngu	calli	calli	watla	u
Maize	ehpe	nahma	centl	centli	aya	—
Rain	unde	coprinumbi	quiavit	quianitl	li	—

38. Cultural and linguistic interrelationships between Central and South America have proved fascinating and perplexing. The hammock, blowgun, and *duho* (n. 98) probably originated in South America, as did the chewing of coca (which came north only as far as Nicaragua). Costa Rican and Honduran languages have South American affiliation. (Strong, 384; Kidder, 444-45, 452-53.)

39. Friedrichsthal (n. 76) described Omotepec Island as two cones of porous granite connected by a two-league isthmus. The 5000-foot western cone was woodland and savanna for two-thirds of its height, and "the atmospheric precipitation on its summit is so great that we were wading deep in mud, and the trees teeming with wet." The island had two towns and its total population was 1700. Friedrichsthal considered all the lake's islands necropolises, because of their many "sepulchres." (Friedrichsthal, 100; Lehmann, 1013.)

40. Julius Froebel (1805-93), a German mineralogist and journalist-politician, toured America 1849-57. The Río Mico may be a tributary of the Escondido, in southern Nicaragua; Bluefields is a town on the Caribbean coast nearby.

41. These Caribs do not seem to be the island people of that name whom the Spaniards considered cannibalistic and suitable only for slaves. (Sauer, 6, 31.)

42. See n. 25.

English	Nagrandan	Chorotegan or Dirian	Niquiran	Mexican	Waikna or Moscan	Woolwa
Flower	—	nele	sochit	xochtli	—	—
Wind	neena	neshtu	hecat	ehecatl	pasa	uing
Snake	apu	nule	coat	coatl	piuta	—
Eagle	—	moonkoyo	oate	quautli	—	—
Flint	eese	nugo	topecat	tecpatl	walpa	—
Mountain	—	diria	tepec	tepec	—	asang
One	imba	teka	ce	ce	kumi	alaslaj
Two	apu	nah	ome	ome	wal	muyebu
Three	asu	ho	ye	yei	niupa	muyebas
Four	acu	hahome	nau	naui	wal wal	muyerunca
Five	hiusu	—	macuil	macuilli	matasip	muyesinca?

Of what I have called *Chorotegan* or *Dirian*, I was only able to procure the vocabulary which is presented on a subsequent page; but of the *Nagrandan*, after much trouble and through the assistance of my friend, Col. Francisco Díaz Zapata,/43/ I obtained some of the grammatical rules and forms of construction, and to this language the following remarks are applicable:

Neither the article nor the preposition is expressed. "The man speaks," *rahpa-data.* "The rage of the dog," *gahu-romoa.* "Dog with rage," *romoa-gahu.* "Beauty of the woman," *musa-rapaku.* "Woman with beauty," *rapaku-musa.*

The plural is formed by adding *nu* to the singular, thus: *ruscu*, bird, *ruscunu*, birds; *eshe*, tree, *eshenu*, trees.

The degrees of comparison seem to have been indicated by prefixes, of which, however, there are but two, equivalent in their signification to "more" and "most," and to "better" and "best." They are *mah*, better or more, *pooru* or *puru*, best or most. For example:

meheña	good
mah-meheña	better-good, or more good
puru-meheña	best good, or most good.

Deficiency or diminution was expressed by *ai* or *mai*, thus: *ai-meheña* or *mai-meheña*, bad, or lacking-good.

Of a man fair of complexion, or what they understand to be of better complexion than another, i.e., a better man, *mah-rahpa.* To run is *dagalnu* or *nagagnu*, and runner is *dagalni*; fast runner, *mah-dagalni*; very fast runner, *puru-dagalni*. *Ahmba*, old; *mah-ahmba* or *ahmba-nu*, older, or more old; *puru-ahmba*, very old. In the Mexican this is effected by reduplication, as *hue*, old, *hue-hue*, old-old, or very old. The word *amba* or *'mba* sometimes has the value of great, and as such it appears in the numerals: thus *diño*, ten, *diñoamba*, great ten, or old ten—i.e. the first power of ten, or one hundred. *Tahi* is small, *chichi*, very small. In the combination of these, and also of *ahmba* or *amba*, as in the Mexican, the final syllable only is used. Thus *egni*, fish, *egnimba*, big fish; *egnihi*, little fish, *egnichi*, very little fish.

The pronouns are as follows:

I	icu	She	icagui	These (m)	cadchinulu
We (m)	hechelu	They (m)	icanu	These (f)	cadchici
We (f)	hecheri	They (f)	icagunu	Mine (m)	cugani
Thou	ica	That	cagui	Mine (f)	icagani
Ye (m)	hechela	Those	caguina	Yours (m)	cutani
Ye (f)	hechelai	This (m)	cala	Yours (f)	icatani
He	icau	This (f)	hala	His	cagani

I could not procure a complete paradigm of any verb. Col. Zapata furnished me with the following, embracing some

43. When he arrived at León Squier made an official speech, whereupon Zapata suddenly stepped forward from the military ranks and recited an "apostrophe" to the U.S. flag (reproduced in Squier). (Squier, i 255.)

of the inflexions of the verbs *sa*, to be, and *aiha*, to come. I am a little skeptical about the accuracy of the future tenses of *sa*:

SA—To Be
Present

SINGULAR			PLURAL	
I am	*sá*		We are	*so*
Thou art	*sá*		Ye are	*soa*
He is	*sá*		They are	*sula*

Imperfect

I was	*caná*		We were	*cananá*
Thou wast	*caná*		Ye were	*cananoá*
He was	*caná*		They were	*lacananá*

Preterite Definite

I was	*sá cá*		We were	*sá cuá*
Thou wast	*sachu*		Ye were	*sá cuahi*
He was	*sa cá*		They were	*sa gahu*

Pluperfect

I had been	*mucasini*		
Thou hadst been	*mucanasini*		(plural the same)
He had been	*mucanasadini*		

Future Absolute

I shall be	*lamauambi*		We shall be	*lamananna*
Thou wilt be	(same)		Ye will be	(same)
He will be	(same)		They will be	*lamana*

Future Anterior

I shall have been	*malamana*		We shall have been	*lamana*
Thou wilt have been	*lama*		Ye will have been	*lamala*
He will have been	*lama*		They will have been	*lamalahi*

AIHA, TIHA, or AHIHA—To Come
Present

I come	*icunaha*		We come	*hechelunagubia*
Thou comest	*icanaha*		Ye come	*hechelaguhala*
He comes	*icannaha*		They come	*icagunuguha*

Imperfect

I did come	*icunahalu*		We did come	*hechelunagubalú*
Thou didst come	*icanahacha*		Ye did come	*hechelanaguabala*
He did come	*icaunahalu*		They did come	*icagunaguhalu*

Perfect

I came	*icusanaha*		We came	*hechelusagualalu*
Thou camest	*icasanacaha*		Ye came	*hechelasagualala*
He came	*icausahalu*		They came	*icaguinasagunhulu*

Pluperfect

I had come	*icuschisalu*		We had come	*hechelunigualalu*
Thou hadst come	*icaschisahala*		Ye had come	*hechelaniguilala*
He had come	*icausahalu*		They had come	*icaguinuschisagunhula*

Future Absolute

I shall come	*icugaha*	We shall come	*hecheluguha*
Thou wilt come	*icaguhacha*	Ye will come	*hechulagualala*
He will come	*icaugaha*	They will come	*icaugnugunhualu*

Future Anterior

I shall have come	*icuvihiluniha*	We shall have come	*hechehivihiluingualalu*
Thou wilt have come	*icavihilunechala*	Ye will have come	*hechulavihilunigula*
He will have come	*icauguivihiluniahalu*	They will have come	*icauinushenguhualu*

Imperative

Come thou	*ahiyaica*	Let us come	*ahiyohecheu*
Let him come	*gahahagui*	Let them come	*gunhuaganeñu*

Conditional Present

I should come	*icugahalu*	We should come	*hechelugualalu*
Thou wouldst come	*icagahachala*	Ye would come	*hechalamagualama*
He would come	*icaugahalu*	They would come	*icauguinumagnuhuama*

Second Conditional Past

If I had come	*icumahaluvihilu*	If we had come	*hechelumainueamaguiha*
If thou hadst come	*icamaimacha*	If ye had come	*hechelamagunhunuma*
If he had come	*icauguimaimaha*	If they had come	*icauguinasohimisaguhua*

I am not prepared to say that the above inflexions are altogether correct; I nevertheless give them as they were communicated to me. I can only add to the above, from my own knowledge:

Daiya	to see	*Dahta*	to speak
Sadaiyama	to have seen	*Dahtanga*	speaking
Daiyanga	seeing		

I have said that the Indians of the Atlantic coast of Nicaragua, the Moscos and others, were probably of Carib stock. This opinion is founded not only upon the express statements of Herrera, who says that "the Carib language was much spoken in Nicaragua," but also upon their general appearance, habits, and modes of life. Their language does not appear to have any direct relationship with that of the Southern Caribs; but is probably the same, or a dialect of the same, with that spoken around what is now called Chiriquí Lagoon,/44/ near the Isthmus of Panama, and which was originally called Chiribiri or Charibici, from which comes Gómera's Caribici or Carib.(1)

The subjoined table comprises a list of about two hundred words in the Nagrandan and Dirian or Chorotegan dialects or languages. I have also added a list of Moscan or Mosquitian words, derived from the copious vocabulary collected by Mr. A. J. Cotheal, in the Second Volume of these *Transactions.*/45/

44. Chiquirí Bay had been discovered by Columbus on his last voyage; he found natives here wearing the first gold jewelry he saw in the New World. (Sauer, 125-26, 131.)

(1) Thirteen leagues from the Gulf of Nicoya (toward the east, doubtless), Oviedo speaks of a village called Carabizi, where the same language was spoken as at Chiriquí. The country on the Pacific, in the same latitude with Chiriquí, was called Cabiores; and next to it was a province called Durucaca; of both of which the inhabitants were barbarous and degraded—whence the Spaniards, in token of their contempt for the Jews, called this section of country "Judea." //Oviedo, Chap. 12.//

45. Alexander J. Cotheal, "A Grammatical Sketch of the Language Spoken by the Indians of the Mosquito Shore." American Ethnological Society, *Transactions*, Vol. 2, 235-64.

English	Nagrandan	Chorotegan or Dirian	Moscan
God	—	gopahemedeo	—
Devil	koonete	nimbumbi	wulasha
Man	rahpa	nuho	waikna
Woman	rapaku	nahseyomo	mairen
Boy	saika	nasome	tukta
Girl	saiku	naheyum	kiki
Child	chichi	naneyame	lupia
Father	ana	gooha	aize
Mother	autu	goomo	yapte
Husband	a'mbin	'mbohue	maia
Wife	a'guyu	nume	maia-mairen
Son	sacule	nasomeyamo	lupia-waikna
Daughter	saicula	nasayme	lupia-mairen
Brother	geneu	mambo	monika
Sister	—	borunyama	laikra
Head	a'cu or edi	goochemo	lel
Hair	tu'su	membe	tanwa
Face	enu	grote	mawan
Forehead	guitu	goola	prurera
Ear	nau	nuhme	kaima
Eye	setu	nahte	nakro
Nose	ta'co	mungoo	kamka
Mouth	dahnu	nunsu	bila
Tongue	duhu	greuhe	twaisa
Tooth	se'mu	nehe	napa
Beard	dambalu	gesagua	unmia
Neck	abulu	—	nana
Arm	pa'pu	deno	klakla
Hand	prechi	—	mita
Fingers	danau	—	sinaia
Nails	senanu	monsa	armala
Body	go'po	booproma	upla
Belly	schambo	goose	biarra
Leg	suntu	geeko	woyata
Foot	naku	graho	mena
Toes	danac'ua	—	mena-senaia
Bone	—	necone	dusa
Heart	buneo	nambooma	kupi
Blood	aite	nenuh	tala
Chief	namede	—	wati
Friend	—	—	uple
House, hut	gua	nahngu	watla
Kettle	daren	—	dikwa
Arrow	—	nitore	trisba
Bow	—	—	pinata
Axe	tlahua	nemoaguya	asa?
Knife	guichulu	—	skiro
Canoe	daguao	—	dore
Bread	upa	—	tane
Tobacco	rande	nemurema	twaka?

English	Nagrandan	Chorotegan or Dirian	Moscan
Sky	dehmalu	nekupe	kasbrica
Moon	—	—	kati
Sun	ahca	numbu	lapta
Star	ucu	nuete	slilma
Day	be or belu	—	iwa
Night	medoun	copripiomu	—
Season	ucumes	—	nani
Year	sigu?	—	—
Wind	nena	neshtu	pasa
Lightning	nagayatu	—	yunmila
Thunder	nadua	—	alwane
Rain	unde	coprinumbi	li
Fire	ahku	nahu	panta
Water	eeia	nimbu	lia
Earth	gooba	nekoopu	tasba
Sea	daneia	nimbuyumbu	kabo
River	eeia	—	awala
Creek	ea-chi	—	tingmi
Island	timbah	—	daukwara
Stone	esee or esenu	nugo	walpa
Maize	eshe	nahma	aya
Wood	barra	nanguima	dus
Leaf	ena	nema	waia
Bark	—	nanzogua	taia
Grass	rana	—	twi
Flesh	nai	nampoome	wina
Deer	—	numbongame	sula
Squirrel	biseaha	—	buteong
Dog	romoa	nambi	yul
Rabbit	—	—	kaiaki
Snake	apu	nule	piuta
Egg	ragha	nuguloge	marbra
Turkey	chimpepe	—	kusu
Fish	egni	pocuguet	inska
White	mesha	andirume	pine
Black	medagina	nansome	siksa
Red	manga	arimbome	paune
Green	masha	—	sane
Small	chichi	nasunge	silpe
Great	oompa	nema	tara
Old	ahmba	nuhyumbe	almuk
Young	datie	nosominyumu	wama
Good	mehena	—	yamne
Bad	aimehena	—	saura
Dead	ganganu	gagame	pruan
I	icu	saho	yung
Thou	ica	sumusheta	ruan
He	ica	—	wetin
We	hechelu	semehmu	yung-nani
Ye	hechela	semehmu	man-nani

English	Nagrandan	Chorotegan or Dirian	Moscan	English	Nagrandan	Chorotegan or Dirian	Moscan
They	icanu	—	wetin-nani	Road	gamba	—	—
This	cala	—	naha	To eat	asu?	—	paiai
That	cagui	—	baha	To drink	mahuia	boprima	daaia
All	duwawa	semehmu	puk	To run	dagalnu	botupu	plap-aia
Many	—	pocope	nia	To leap	masiga	boora	soutw-aia
Much	—	—	nia	To come	aiho	aroya?	bal-aia
Who	—	—	dia	To go	aiyu or icu	paya	waia
Near	inge	—	lama	To sing	nagamo	pacoondamu	aiwnuaia
Today	endola	yazra	na-iua	To sleep	ami	payacope	yap-aia
Yesterday	deshe	—	iua-wala	To speak	dahta	mage?	ais-aia
Tomorrow	gase	paseanyaro	yunka	To see	daiya	oome	kaik-aia
Yes	mena	—	au?	To kill	maharega	koypame	ik-aia?
No	unta	aco	ahia	To love	nanjawala	—	—
Buttock	gashtug	—	—	To ask	danda	—	—
Bird	pusku	—	—	To take	aaya	—	—
A fly	ñug	—	—	To keep silent	pruisha	—	—
Above	purumicita	—	—	To know	daininu	—	—
Silver	prahea	—	—	To die	neageña	—	—
Plantain	numbaba	—	—	Temple	—	nangumba	—
Word	enita	—	—	Mountain	—	diria	—
Basket	dashtu	—	—	Cave	—	nu'pe	—
Hot	tehsmica	—	—	Smoke	—	nemare	—
Warm	mica	—	—	Flower	—	nele	—
Breeches	frela	—	—	Reed	—	nure	—
Hat	gadusi	—	—	Eagle	—	moonkoyo	—
Ox	auha	—	—	Lake	—	neenda	—
Fever	ganguiga	—	—	Afternoon	—	tasipio	—

The word for *man* in the Moscan language is *Waikna*,/46/ and *Waikna* is the name which the Moscan Indians, before their debasement by intermixture with the Negroes, arrogated to themselves. It was a very common practice, among the aborigines of America, to distinguish their tribe by a word meaning "the Men," *par excellence.* This is the significance of the name *Apache*, borne by the roving Indians of northern Mexico. With the Athapascas, *dennee*, the Algonkins and others, *inne*, with the Muyscans, *muysca*, and with the Araucanians, *reche*, all signified *the men*, or pure men, and entered into the designations of the various tribes./47/

Subjoined is the vocabulary, procured by Mr. Froebel, in Chontales, and referred to above. As there observed, it does not seem to have any affinity with the other Nicaraguan languages, except a faint relationship in the inflexions of the verb with the Nagrandan.

46. Squier chose this word for the title of his book, *Waikna: or Adventures on the Mosquito Shore* (New York: Harpers, 1855). It was written pseudonymously "by Samuel A. Bard" so he could freely criticize British policy in the Mosquito area.

47. The Apaches were frequently raiders of the more docile southwestern Pueblo Indians. Athapascan refers to westerly North American tribes of common linguistic stock, in contradistinction to Algonkian tribes to the east. The Algonkins (or Algonquins) inhabited the St. Laurence Valley. The Muyscas are native to Colombia. For Araucanians, see n. 51.

WOOLWA

Sun	*māa*	Sister	*amini*	To sleep	*amacuting*
Day	*māada*	Head	*tunni*	To eat	*tecuting*
Star	*māabka*	Arm	*uacálni*	I am	*acaralaúyang*
Moon	*uáigo*	Foot	*cálni*	Thou art	*ayalalaúga*
Fire	*cuh*	Eye	*miniktaka*	He is	*alaslaúga*
Water	*wass*	Nose	*nágnitak*	We are	*yaralalauca*
Earth	*sāno*	Mouth	*dinibas*	Ye are	*laucayalálanca*
Night	*baraca*	Blood	*anasscá*	They are	*eauyoadá*
Air, wind	*uing*	House	*ū*	1	*alosláj*
Mountain	*asang*	Town	*uálna*	2	*muyebu*
Man	*all*	Plantain	*uagi*	3	*muyebas*
Woman	*yall*	Sugar	*disnok*	4	*muyarunca*
Father	*papāni?*	Cow	*sana*	5	*muyesinca?*
Mother	*mamani?*	Milk	*sanadagoscá*	6	*dijca* or *muydijca*
Son	*paunima*	Horse	*pomca*	7	*bajca* or *muybajca*
Daughter	*paucoma*	Tiger	*nágua*	8	*muyacca*
Little boy	*tiguis*	Dog	*sulo*	9	*yaccabavo*
Little girl	*batanil*	Cat	*nisto*	10	*muyhasluy*
Brother	*uajaini*	Fish	*tabomm*		

So far as can be ascertained, the Indians of Nicaragua practiced a system of numeration corresponding with that common to nearly all the civilized, and some of the barbarous, nations of the continent. That is to say, they used what Mr. Gallatin/48/ has denominated the *vigintesimal system*, instead of the decimal—i.e., counted by twenties instead of tens. Among the Eskimos,/49/ the Algonkins, the Choctaws, and some other nations and families, it seems that the primitive method of counting was by fives. This is what may be called *finger-counting*; and that their system of numbers originated in counting first the fingers of one hand, then of both, and finally both fingers and toes, is established by the names of the numerals themselves.

The word expressing the number 5, in the Carib of Essequibo,/50/ the Moscan, and some other languages, means *one hand*; that expressing 10, *two hands*, or both hands; that expressing 20, *a man*, i.e., both hands and feet. In the Eskimo, 8, 9, and 10 respectively mean the middle, the fourth, and little finger.(2) The Peruvians/51/ and Araucanians had a purely decimal system. Humboldt/52/ has shown that the vigintesimal system existed in the Basque—that enigmatical language which seems to hold more and closer affinities to some of those of America than any known to have existed in the Old World.

48. Albert Gallatin (1761-1849), Swiss-born linguist and ethnologist and U.S. statesman, wrote on the mound builders and on Mexican civilizations. As president of the American Ethnological Society he encouraged much exploratory work—including Squier's—in Central America. The word "vigintesimal" (counting by twenties—now vigesimal) was apparently his creation.

49. The Eskimos occupy the Arctic coasts of America and Russia; they are the only race native to both Old and New Worlds. The Choctaws were a large tribe living chiefly in Mississippi; they were called "Flatheads" because they compressed the heads of male infants; see also n. 67. (Latham 1850, 288-94.)

50. The Essequibo is a river in British Guiana (South America). For Moscan, the language of the Moscos, see n. 19.

(2) Crantz says of the Eskimos, "Their proper numeral table is *five*; then counting on their fingers they call *six* by the name of the first finger, and for the following repeat two, three, four, five; and count from ten to twenty with their toes. Sometimes, instead of twenty they say '*a man*'; for one hundred, '*five men.*' " //David Crantz (or Cranz, 1723-77), a Moravian missionary, worked in Greenland; he wrote a history of Greenland published in 1765.//

51. Squier's "Peruvians" were the Incas (see also n. 96). The Araucanians (or Araucans) are primitive non-Incan Indians living in Chile and Argentina whom the Incas had subjugated.

52. Alexander von Humboldt (1769-1859), German naturalist, traveler, and statesman, made a scientific journey to South America and Mexico (1799-1804), where he studied the climate and other earth sciences, etc., on which he published copiously. The Basques (below) are people of northern Spain whose origins have never been fully explained.

I was able to procure the complete numerals of only the Nagrandan dialect or language. They are given below. It will be observed that there is a simple, uncompounded word for *ten*, and another for *twenty*.

1	imba	1	10	guha	10	19	guanmelnu	10+9
2	apu	2	11	guanimba	10+1	20	dino, imbadiño, or 'badiño	1 x 20
3	asu	3	12	guanapu	10+2	21	'badiñoimbanu	1 x 20 + 1
4	acu	4	13	guanasu	10+3	22	'badiñoapunu	1 x 20 + 2
5	huisu	5	14	guanacu	10+4	23	'badiñoasunu	1 x 20 + 3
6	mahu	6	15	guanisu	10+5	30	'badiñoguhanu	1 x 20 + 10
7	niquinu	7	16	guanmahu	10+6	31	'badiñoguanimbanu	1 x 20 + 10 + 1
8	nuha	8	17	guanquinu	10+7	32	'badiñoguanapunu	1 x 20 + 10 + 2
9	melnu	9	18	guanuha	10+8	33	'badiñoguanasunu	1 x 20 + 10 + 3

40	apudiño	2 x 20	70	asudiñogubanu	3 x 20 + 10
41	apudiñoimbanu	2 x 20 + 1	80	acudiño	4 x 20
42	apudiñoapunu	2 x 20 + 2	90	acudiñoguhanu	4 x 20 + 10
43	apudiñoasunu	2 x 20 + 3	100	huisudiño or guhamba	5 x 20 or great 10
50	apudiñoguhanu	2 x 20 + 10	200	guahadiño	10 x 20
51	apudiñoguanimbanu	2 x 20 + 10 + 1	400	diñoamba	great 20
52	apudiñoguanapunu	2 x 20 + 10 + 2	1000	guhaisudiño	10 x 5 x 20
60	asudiño	3 x 20	2000	huisudiñoamba	5 great 20's
			4000	guhadiñoamba	10 great 20's

The terminal *amba* or *mba* in the Nagrandan language signified great or increase; one hundred, therefore, is sometimes called *guhamba*, or great ten; *diñoamba*, or great twenty, is four hundred; and ten great twenties is four thousand. In common, I believe, with the Maya only, the Nagrandan words for 40, 60, 80, 100, etc., mean respectively twice twenty, three, four, and five times twenty. In common also with the Maya, the numerals from 20 to 39 are compounded of 20 and the numerals from one to nineteen, with the addition of the terminal *nu*, which is the sign of the plural. But in the Maya this terminates with 40, while in the Nagrandan it is continued throughout, from 40 to 60, 60 to 80, etc.

Col. Galindo/53/ has given us the names of six tribes of Indians in Costa Rica, of none of which have we any vocabularies. Neither have we any of the languages spoken in San Salvador and in Honduras. There is reason to believe, however, that the Chondal extended into the latter state, as also the language spoken on the coast. It is also probable that the language which I have called the Nagrandan prevailed among the aborigines occupying the salubrious central plateau of Honduras. This I infer from the names of Chinandega,/54/ Posultega, Chichigalpa, Comogalpa, on the plain of León, and Matagalpa, Tegucigalpa, etc., which are clearly from one source, on the plateau of Honduras.

In Guatemala there existed a variety of languages or dialects, stated at eighteen and at twenty-four, of which the Poconchí,/55/ the Quiché, Quichekiel or Kachiquiel, Sinca, Chortí, Mam, and Subtugil were the principal. The vocabularies of none of these, so far as we are enabled to institute comparisons, sustain any relation to those of Nicaragua.

That the Niquirans were Mexicans requires no further or better proof than is afforded by the fragments of their language already presented. The fact, as we have seen, was distinctly asserted by the early voyagers; but as they did not

53. John Galindo (or Juan, 1802-1840?), an Irishman, went to Central America and in the new Guatemalan republic became governor of the Petén. He publicized the area's archaeological wonders, especially neighboring Palenque, in short notices sent to various scientific journals.

54. These towns have Niquiran names; Posuetega also appears as Poçoltega, Pozoltega (Lehmann, 1008.)

55. For Poconchí, Quiché, Quichekiel or Kachiquiel (sic—both referring to Cakchiquel), and Mam, see n. 35. The Sinca language (also Lenca or Xincan) of Guatemala and Honduras is still not clearly known. Chortí, also called Apay, is the language of the Chols of Guatemala. Subtugil or Tzutujil is also called Achí. (Mason, 60, 73-74.)

present any evidence in support of their statement it never received full credit among students. Indeed, as late as 1850 Dr. Latham,/56/ in his erudite work *The Varieties of Man*, regards the evidence on this point as "by no means conclusive." In completing the evidence and establishing incontestably that such a colony did exist in Nicaragua at the period of Discovery in the fifteenth century, I have the satisfaction of fixing one more and a very important point of departure in American ethnological inquiries; important, as showing that this continent has not been exempt from those migrations, corresponding to the currents and tides of the ocean, which have, earlier or later, swept over every part of the Old World and affected so remarkably, by intermixture and change of soil and climate, the conditions and relations of its inhabitants.

We have then presented to us the extraordinary phenomenon of a fragment of a great aboriginal nation, widely separated from the parent stock, and intruded among other and hostile nations; yet, from the comparative lateness of the separation, or some other cause, still retaining its original, distinguishing features so as to be easily recognized. The causes which led to their migration from Mexico can probably never be accurately known. They have a tradition that they came from the northwest; and that they left their original seats in consequence of having been overpowered by a hostile nation superior to themselves in numbers who, not satisfied with conquering them in battle, made slaves of them, sacrificed their women and children, and outraged them in various ways. They called the country from whence they came Ticomega Emaguatega,/57/ which name corresponds with none with which we are acquainted.

This tradition receives strong support from Torquemada,/58/ who states it as a historical fact, current in Mexico itself, that at a very early period two considerable Mexican nations dwelling in Soconusco, on the coast of Oaxaca, near Tehuantepec, were attacked by the Ulmeques,/59/ who had been their enemies before their settlement in that region —leaving the inference that there had been an anterior migration of the same nations, probably from the valley of Anahuac./60/ The Ulmeques subdued them, imposed on them the most grievous burdens, and sacrificed numbers of them to the gods. Reduced to despair, they consulted their priests, who directed them to depart from the country —which they did, going southward. These, he adds, after various adventures arrived in Nicaragua, where they were well received by the people who made room for them on the shores of the lake. They afterwards extended their limits by war and alliances.*

Fragments, Torquemada adds, dropped off from the main body in Guatemala, where they built Mictlán/61/ (City of

56. Robert G. Latham (1812-88), English ethnologist and philologist, studied the peoples of Europe, England, and the British colonies. His *The Natural History of the Varieties of Man* and *Man and His Migrations* (see Bibliography) furnished Squier much of his data here on various Indian tribes.

57. See n. 120.

58. Fray Juan de Torquemada (1545?-1600) in Mexico City was a Franciscan historian; he saw Hebrew origins in the American Indians. He wrote *Los Viente i un Libros Rituales i Monarchía Indiana . . .*, 3 Vols. (Madrid: 1615).

59. Sic—Olmecs; indigenous peoples of the Veracruz area, their culture and art styles flourished from 1200 to 800 B.C. Their descendants appear to be the cruel masters whose tyranny forced the Nicaraguans to migrate, although the subjugation occurred in the Chiapas area. Except for a few isolated references, the Olmecs were almost unrecognized until the 1930's, when the name "Olmecs" ("Rubber people") became common. (Davies, 118-19; Bernal, 177-80, 189.)

60. According to Davies, "Anahuac" was not normally associated by the chroniclers with the valley of Mexico but with the littorals of the Gulf of Mexico and the Pacific Ocean. Torquemada described the Nicaraguas as "those of Anahuac," probably meaning the Gulf coast. (Davies, 118-19.)

*In another part of his *History*, Torquemada gives an account of a pretended conquest of Nicaragua by Montezuma, in which, however, are mixed up the same circumstances elsewhere related as connected with the migration; showing, as observed by M. Ternaux-Compans, that it is only the old tradition, applied to modern times.

61. Mictlán or Mitlán (from N. *mic, miqui*, death, *tlan*, region, place), "City of the dead," probably originated as a name at several sites when Indians found signs of extinct habitation. This occurred at Mitla, near Oaxaca in Mexico, and at Mita, now Asunción Mita and Santa Catarina Mita, in Guatemala. See also n. 117.

Yzcuitlán, Squier's "City of the Rabbit," is today Escuintla, Guatemala. Díaz del Castillo called it Escueta, derived from (N.) Itzcuintlán. But the word *izcuint* means "dog," and only secondarily other small animals like the tepezcuinte ("mountain dog"—the agouti or paca) or the rabbit. "Rabbit" in Nahuatl is *tochtli*; see n. 148.

the Dead) and Yzcuitlán (City of the Rabbit), and where there still exist numerous places bearing names of Mexican origin. Among the migrating tribes he mentions the Cholultecas as separating from the rest and settling on the Gulf of Nicoya. He probably means to say the Gulf of Fonseca, where, as we have seen, the name is still perpetuated. This opinion is supported by his subsequent declaration that one portion of the people among whom the Mexicans intruded themselves fled to Nicoya, thus accounting for the division of the Chorotegans already referred to. Torquemada also states that the Mexicans founded a city on Lake Managua which they called Xolotlán,/62/ or in the Chorotegan language, Nagrando. But if so, it seems most likely that they afterwards abandoned the position. Had they held it at the time of the Conquest the fact would not have escaped Oviedo.

It has been supposed that the Pipil Indians,/63/ occupying the coast of San Salvador, were also of Mexican origin and arrived in Central America at the same time with the colony in Nicaragua. We have no vocabulary of their language, but the names of most of the places in the region which they occupied—or occupy—are clearly Mexican. Istepec, Usulután, Sesuntepec, Cuscutlán, Suchiltepec, Cojutepec, Cuyutitán, Jilpango, etc., are unmistakably Mexican. It has, however, been suspected that the friendly Indians from Mexico who accompanied Alvarado/64/ in his conquest of the country were established here, and that the names to which I have referred were given by them. This is a point which is yet open to investigation; meantime, I incline to the belief that a Mexican colony also existed in San Salvador.

The Mexican historian Ixtlixochitl/65/ records that at the period of the destruction of the Toltecan Empire,/66/ in the year Cetecpatl, or 959 of our era, a part of those who survived went to the southward, to Nicaragua. But the traditions of the people themselves indicate that the recital of Torquemada is nearest the truth. It seems, therefore, that this colony, like that of the Mormons in the Valley of the Salt Lake, and that of the Jews in Palestine, was founded by a general migration undertaken in consequence of persecutions, through the midst of intervening nations—an armed migration, giving war to the weak and the hostile, and negotiating with the friendly. It is serious and important to know of an authentic instance where migrations of this kind have taken place on this continent, in estimating the possible as well as the probable relationship which may exist between its various families.

That similar separations and migrations have occurred in the night of American history seems undoubted; but at periods so remote that offshoots have lost their original features or have retained them in a modified and obscured form painful to the investigator, because suggestive of relations which it is impossible clearly to establish. We have a remarkable example in the Natchez,/67/ a small tribe on the Mississippi River, whose institutions, civil and religious, manners, habits, and customs approximated closely to the Peruvians; more closely, in fact, than to any other nation of the continent. Enigmatical fragments like these, scattered over both the Northern and Southern Hemispheres, betoken a high antiquity for the American race.

The causes which led to these separations, and the motives which impelled the American nations to divisions and migrations, must probably remain forever unknown, except so far as they may be inferred from the recorded history of the Old World. For, after all, man, of whatever race or however situated, is subject to the same laws and guided by the

62. The Cholultecas (Torquemada's spelling—Cholulteca and Choroteca are versions of the same word) had no direct connection with Cholulá (n. 120) but were from Xolotlán (Chiapas). Xolotlán, Cholotla, etc., was a common place name, repeated again in Nicaragua (below). For Nagrando see n. 27. (Davies, 117-18.)

63. The Pipil ("children," "nobles"), Nahua speakers from Tula (n. 66), settled in Guatemala and Nicaragua via Cholulá. The Nicaráo, a Pipil group, reached Nicaragua, bringing many Mexican customs; see n. 23. (Wolf, 42, 121.)

64. Pedro de Alvarado (1495?-1541) as a Spanish soldier fought with Cortés in Mexico and in 1523-27 led an expedition to conquer Guatemala. He then governed there 1530-34.

65. Sic—see n. 82.

66. Tula, or Tollan, in Hidalgo (Mexico), had been the home of the Toltecs. About 800 A.D. ancestors of the Pipil (n. 63) left Tula, as did the Nicaráo (n. 23). By the time of its collapse (not in *Ce tecpal*, "One flint," nor Sahagún's 1110, but more likely in Davies' 1179 A.D.) many Tula people had resettled throughout southern Mexico and Central America. (Wolf, 111-17, 120-24; Davies, 466.)

67. The Natchez occupied Mississippi River areas around the present city of that name. Their characteristics included flattened head, sun worship, a matriarchal caste system, human sacrifice, and maintenance of an "undying" fire. Latham had called these "Mexican" traits, but Squier strangely associates them with the "Peruvian" Incas. (Latham 1851, 120.)

same influences. The state of separation—*disruption*, as it is sometimes called—in which the American race was found, has been variously attributed to a radical physiological defect in its character, to extraordinary natural phenomena, convulsions of nature, such as are said to have swallowed up the island of Atalantis—calamities filling men with a terror so monstrous that, handed down from race to race, it darkened their intellects and hardened their hearts and drove them, flying from each other, far from the blessings of social life. To me, however, this separation and subdivision of the aboriginal race, and the exclusion of its different families, in respect to each other, seem rather due to long periods of time and long continued migrations of single nations and tribes from one portion of the continent to the other.

The discoverers, when they landed on the shores of our own country, found one great current of migration setting from the northwest upon the region now occupied by the New England and Middle States. Another flowed from the direction of Texas and New Mexico into the Southern States east of the Mississippi; and the slow but constant southward tendency of the Oregon tribes/68/ has been a frequent subject of remark among observers. I do not now refer to those traces of vast populations antedating all traditions which abound in the Mississippi Valley, mute but most truthful and impressive witnesses of ancient migrations—not of single tribes and petty nations, but of vast families of men.

The causes of these migrations, as I have said, must probably remain conjectural. It is the popular belief that most have been from the north toward the south; and the plausible explanation, that more genial climates and fertile soils were the impelling causes to them, has been generally accepted. Yet, like many other popular beliefs, it is eminently unfounded. The great tides of men have flowed very nearly upon the same parallels of latitude. The descent of the Germans on Rome was no migration, as compared with these; it was the eddy, the outward flow of the great current, which afterwards swept over the ocean barrier, traversed a new world, and is now gathering its volumes on the golden shores of the Pacific./69/

MONUMENTS AND RELICS OF ART

Our knowledge of the antiquities of Central America extends only to those found in the northern portion of that interesting—but as yet little known—country; and is confined to the monuments at Copán,/70/ in Honduras, and Quiriguá and Quiché or Quezaltenango, in Guatemala. The researches of Messrs. Stephens/71/ and Catherwood, in conjunction with a few incidental notices from Galindo and others, have made these familiar to the world and excited the deepest interest as to the results of future investigations. The extent of population and the degree of civilization which they indicate have naturally led to the conclusion that many others exist in the same regions, the discovery of which will reward the adventurous explorer and throw new light upon the primitive civilization of the New World.

But in prosecuting researches here, there are many difficulties to be encountered which can be but imperfectly estimated by those not on the spot. The population of Central America is small and almost entirely confined to certain narrow localities upon the Pacific slope; and the political circumstances of the people, as well as the state of education among them, have been such as to afford little encouragement to archaeological studies. As a consequence, they know far less than the people of the United States of the aboriginal monuments of their own vicinity. Little information of

68. Latham had characterized Oregon as an area of undeveloped agriculture. The tribes were the Salish, Piskwaus, Wallawallahs, Skitsuish, and others. (Latham 1850, 313-14.)

69. Squier appears to see in the 1848 California gold rush a continuation of German vandalization—John Sutter (1803-80) had been a German emigre. (Squier had just written "Gold Hunting in California, in the Sixteenth Century." *American Review*, January 1849, 84-88.)

70. Copán and its satellite Quiriguá, flourishing about 700 A.D., indeed contain the most spectacular of all carved lowland Maya stelae. Highland Guatemala's Quezaltenango was actually the home of the Mam Maya (n. 55), while the nearby Quiché (n. 35), flourishing about 1300 A.D., were centered at Santa Cruz del Quiché. The highland sites today have almost no "monuments" beyond massive temple foundations.

71. John L. Stephens (1805-52), an American lawyer, had traveled throughout Europe, Egypt, and Arabia, writing popular accounts. With Catherwood as his artist he reached Copán in 1839. Frederick Catherwood (d. 1854), an architect, had sketched antiquities in Egypt and the Near East before accompanying Stephens on his Yucatán and Central American expeditions.

importance to the investigator can be gathered from them. Besides, by far the greater proportion of the country is in its primitive state and covered with dense, tangled, and almost impenetrable tropical forests, rendering fruitless all attempts at systematic investigation.

There are vast tracts untrodden by human feet, or traversed only by Indians, who have a superstitious reverence for the moss-covered and crumbling monuments that are hidden in the depths of the wilderness, and which their vague traditions tell them are remnants of the greatness of their fathers, the shrines and statues of their ancient gods, which it is a religious duty to hide from the profane intrusion of an alien race. These Indians are often unfriendly; and it is only at the risk of life that advances can be made into their fastness. From them but little can be gathered; and if any discoveries are made, it must be by accident. The hunter or the herdsman may encounter ancient remains in the wilderness; and if they are remarkable, or he is curious, he may mark the spot and be able to point it out to the traveler. But the information he may be able to give is always of an uncertain character and leaves the inquirer, if not in actual doubt as to the existence of anything worthy of his attention, at least under the apprehension that, even after a long and fatiguing journey, and after enduring every kind of hardship, he may be unable to discover the object of his search. For these and other reasons it will be long before the treasures of the past which exist in Central America can become fully known. Their investigation must be the gradual work of time, in which individuals can but partially assist.

Most of the monuments which fell under my notice in Nicaragua have been described in my work on that country,/72/ to which, from the impossibility of presenting here the illustrations necessary for their comprehension, the investigator is respectfully referred. They may be described as consisting, for the most part, of ruined *teocallis*,/73/ and monoliths, sustaining a general resemblance to those found at Copán, but smaller and less elaborately ornamented. They are boldly sculptured from the hardest material—generally basalt—and seem designed to represent divinities, strongly distinguished from each other in their attributes, as well as material, or rather symbolical, forms.

In respect to their probable origin, little need be said. They may differ somewhat among themselves in antiquity, for it is not to be supposed that they were all made at the same period. But there is no good reason for supposing that they were not made by the nations found in possession of the country. It is well known that these nations had idols of stone in their temples, which were carved of different forms to represent the various divinities worshiped by their makers. These temples were structures of wood, surrounded by altars, or high places of earth and stone; upon which, as in Mexico, sacrifices were performed. Many of these temples were burned by the conquerors; the high places destroyed, and the idols broken in pieces. And I have had frequent occasion to remark that by far the greater proportion of the monuments yet remaining bear indubitable marks of the conquerors' religious zeal, in their battered faces and broken limbs.

It may seem somewhat incongruous that while Nicaragua was inhabited by people of different families—the autochthones and the intruders from Mexico—their monuments should have sustained so close a resemblance. But while the fact that they differed wholly in language, and greatly in manners and customs, is affirmed by the early chroniclers, the additional fact that they were alike, or closely assimilated, in religion, is also as distinctly asserted.

The monuments found on the island of Zapatero,/74/ in Lake Nicaragua, which there is every reason to believe was occupied by the Niquirans, differ only in size, and their more elaborate workmanship, from those found at Momo-

72. See Bibliography (1852). Stansifer has pointed out that neither in the book nor in this *Transaction* article does Squier endeavor to analyze the statues. (Stansifer, 170-72.)

73. See n. 122.

74. The larger Lake Nicaragua contains Ometepec (n. 39) and Zapatero islands. Precolumbian burials in shoe-shaped clay vessels gave Zapatero ("Shoemaker") its name. In December 1849 Squier visited a cluster of mounds on Zapatero and had his artist, James McDonough, draw the statues. The sculptures generally depict human figures with animals on their backs enclosing the human head in their open jaws. These so-called "alter ego" figures were made famous by McDonough's drawings, since no photographs were taken. Some thought they had Maya origins, but they are now considered a local conception. Squier also had ten pieces shipped to the Smithsonian Institution, Washington, D.C.

Momotombito is in Lake Managua; Livingston (n. 75) and Squier spent a day exploring the island and found more statues, still revered by the Indians. He shipped the largest of them to the Smithsonian also. For Subtiaba, see n. 36.

(Squier, i 245, 302-303, 452-53; ii 41-42, 58; Stansifer, 168-69; Healy, 340; Radell, 22; Lothrop 1973, 181-82; Deuel, 158, 163.)

tombito, Subtiaba, and other places a hundred and fifty miles distant. Monoliths appear to have been common to all the semi-civilized nations of North America.

Among the most remarkable remains in Nicaragua of which I heard, but was prevented from visiting, are the traces of immense works in the district of Chontales, near the Indian town of Juygalpa, on the northern shore of Lake Nicaragua, nearly opposite the city of Granada./75/ They were observed by Dr. Livingston in a visit to the gold mines of that region; and are described by him as consisting of trenches three or four yards broad at the bottom, and extending indefinitely, in a right line, across the savannas, and into the depths of the forest. He followed one for upwards of a mile. At intervals the trenches widen, forming elliptical sunken areas sixty or eighty feet in diameter.

In one of these areas, and on a line transversely to that of the trench, were two small mounds of stone; in the next area four mounds, and so on, alternately. These mounds were five or six feet in height and placed with the utmost regularity. The purposes of these singular remains, as well as their extent, until further and complete investigation, must remain matters of conjecture. It may nevertheless be observed that there are traditions of a ruined city, with a variety of singular monuments, near Juygalpa, of which it may be worth the trouble of the adventurous explorer to determine the truth. It is very certain that the late Chevalier Friedrichsthal/76/ obtained some monuments from the northern shore of the lake—but their fate is unknown.

In my visit to the volcano of Las Pilas, in what was anciently the populous province of Marabios,/77/ about twenty miles northeast of León, and near the base of the volcano of Orota, I was shown a number of low mounds of earth and stone, rectangular, and set round the edges with stones, which seemed to have been the sites or foundations of ancient buildings. They were covered and surrounded by fragments of broken pottery. It is possible that they indicated burial places; but I had no means of excavating them to determine the fact.

In Honduras, as also in San Salvador, I heard of remains and monuments equal to those of Copán in extent and interest, which I had no opportunity of visiting, but which I hope to be able to investigate in person, at no very remote period.

PRIMITIVE CONDITION

In nearly all that relates to the habits, customs, social and civil organization, and religious notions and practices of the Indians of Nicaragua, we are compelled to rely upon the often vague and sometimes contradictory accounts of the early Spanish adventurers and travelers. The fullest and most reliable chronicle is that of Gonzales Hernández de Oviedo y Valdez,/78/ historiographer of the Indies to the King of Spain, who visited Nicaragua in 1526, within four years after its discovery by Gil Gonzáles de Avila./79/ Some portions of his account were used by Herrera in the compilation of his

75. Ruins just north of Granada were the site of Nindiri (Oviedo's Tenderi). A cazique there told Oviedo he often went to the top of nearby Masaya Volcano (n. 28), where an old woman, entirely naked, came out of the crater to make predictions. Joseph Livingston was U.S. consul in León. (Squier, i 223.)

76. Emanuel Ritter von Friedrichsthal (1809-42), naturalist and traveler, toured Central America 1837-41. In a short report (see Bibliography) he referred to ancient towns, temples, and idols "half buried in the soil," but—despite Squier's comment—he did not mention taking anything.

77. Squier's province of Marabios involves the area about Subtiaba (n. 36). Maribio is the name of the language spoken there: it is related to Tlapanec in Guerrero (Mexico) and—strangely enough, as established by Lehmann—to Hokan-speaking tribes in California. (Mason, 61.)

78. Gonzalo Fernández de Oviedo y Valdés (1478-1557) came to America in 1514. He served as overseer and was later appointed historian by Charles V. In 1526 he visited the Nahuatls and Chorotegas of Nicaragua, whose customs he recorded. His *Historia general y natural de las Indias* (first part published 1535, second part 1557) received the Emperor's approval and became immensely popular. (Sauer, xii, 170, 176.)

79. Gil González de Avila (or Dávila, d. 1526—not to be confused with Pedrarias, n. 16), governor of Honduras 1524-25, had earlier explored Panama. In a long expedition up the west coast of Nicaragua (1522-23) he met Nicaráo (n. 23), whose 9000 followers were baptized in one day. Further north 12,600 also accepted Christianity, but another cazique with a large army next drove the Spaniards to ships waiting in the Gulf of Nicoya. The expedition nevertheless returned with 89,000 pesos of gold and claimed to have baptized 29,442. As a conquistador Gil González was unusually gentle. (HMAI, xiii 101; Radell, 55-58.)

History of Spanish America,/80/ who seems also to have had access to some other sources of information with which we are unacquainted. Oviedo's chronicle was, nevertheless, never published in the original; nor does its existence appear to have been known until 1839, when it was discovered by that indefatigable scholar, M. Ternaux-Compans,/81/ who procured a copy of the MS. from Spain and translated and published it in his invaluable series of *Original Voyages and Relations concerning America.*

Besides the accounts of Oviedo, and the detached, compiled chapters of Herrera, we have some references to the aborigines of Nicaragua in Torquemada's *Monarquia Indiana*, in the history of D. Carlos de Alva Ixtlixochitl,/82/ and in the latter work of Gage,/83/ published in 1680. Don Andreas Cerezeda,/84/ who accompanied Gil Gonzáles de Avila as King's Treasurer when he penetrated into Nicaragua in 1522, communicated the outlines of the expedition, with some account of the country and its inhabitants, to Peter Mártyr,/85/ which were incorporated by him in the third and fourth chapters of the sixth of his celebrated *Decades.*

CIVIL, POLITICAL, AND SOCIAL ORGANIZATION, MANNERS, AND CUSTOMS

The Indians of Nicaragua were divided into numerous distinct tribes and petty sovereignties, governed by independent chiefs or caziques./86/ These, it is presumed, were hereditary; but whether the descent was by the female side, as in many other parts of America, or by the male, we are not informed. This condition of things must have resulted in collisions between the several caziques, and by war, intrigue, and alliances, in the aggrandizement of one at the expense of the other. Such was the fact; and by these means some of the chiefs became very powerful and had, as tributaries and vassals, chiefs who were themselves proprietors of villages and districts of land. These were the personal attendants and bodyguards of the greater chiefs, "their captains and courtiers."

We are, however, told that some of the districts and their inhabitants were not governed by caziques but by councils of old men called *guegues*,* in whom were centered the supreme administrative and executive powers./87/ They were elective; and in them was vested the appointment of a military leader, or "war chief," as he was called among the northern nations, who, by virtue of his office was a member of the council. He was, nevertheless, jealously watched,

80. Antonio de Herrera (or Herrara) y Tordesillas (1559-1625), chronicler of the Indies, based his *Historia General* on the writings of Las Casas, Landa, et al., describing the years 1492 to about 1554.

81. Henri Ternaux-Compans (1807-64), a French bibliographer, collected and described early American documents from the Spanish archives. He got them, said Bancroft, "in some unexplained way, possibly . . . //during// the French campaign on the //Iberian// peninsula." Between 1836 and 1840 he published 20 volumes of these manuscripts (in French). (Bernal; Bancroft, i 200.)

82. Sic—Fernando de Alva Cortés Ixtlilxóchitl (1568?-1648), a Mexican historian, had been a descendant of the kings of Texcoco. For Torquemada (above) see n. 58.

83. Fray Thomas Gage (1603-56), an English Dominican traveling in the New World, remained at Verapaz for 12 years to assist in the conversion of Indians there. His account is somewhat biased against the Spanish government.

84. Andreas de Cerezada (or Cereceda) was the King's representative on Gil Gonzaléz de Avila's entrada through Central America (n. 79). He brought the expedition's gold back to Spain and wrote a relación of the event.

85. Peter Mártyr d'Anghiera (1457-1526), Italian historian and royal chronicler at the Spanish court, wrote *De Orbe novo decades octo* (Seville: 1530 etc.) and with supplements described America's discovery decade by decade.

86. See n. 2.

*This I take to be a Mexican word, formed by the reduplication of *hue* or *gue*, old, *huehue*, or *guegue*, literally "old-old," i.e. very old. *Huehue*-tlalapán, the Very-old-tlalapán, and Gueguetenango, Very-old-tenango, are names of places both in Mexico and Guatemala. //Squier has shortened Oviedo's *huehuetlatolli* (N. hue, old, *tlatolli*, talk), "council" of elders. (León-Portilla, 68, 80; Molina.)//

87. Oviedo and other early Spaniards in Central America, by calling the native leaders *caziques* (chiefs), have implied the presence of chiefdoms. Among modern anthropologists the chiefdom is reserved for socially and politically centralized societies composed of economically interdependent communities, whereas the tribe is a less sophisticated self-contained group of culturally similar people. It now appears, especially for lower Central America, that there were more tribes than chiefdoms. The council of elders indicates a lack of strong central leadership. See Creamer and Haas.

and if suspected of plotting against the safety of the commonwealth, or for the purpose of securing supreme power in his own hands, was rigorously put to death by the council of *guegues*. These councils were early abolished by the Spaniards, "who found it easier to control one man than a number," each one of whom had equal influence among the people. The *guegues* were also the chroniclers of their respective tribes, and made books in which they recorded their boundaries and the limits of property, "with all the rivers, lakes, and forests, to which reference was made in case of dispute among their own people, or with the other tribes."

The custom of tattooing, it seems, was practiced to a certain extent, at least so far as to designate, by peculiarities in the marks, the several tribes or caziques to which the people belonged. "For," says Oviedo, "both sexes pierce their ears and make drawings on their bodies with stone knives, which are rendered black and permanent by a kind of coal called *tile*."/88/

The local administrations differed very much, according to the temper of the cazique. There nevertheless were many well established rules by which he was governed that were seldom or never violated. The nature of some of these will be discovered as we proceed. The subordinate officers of the caziques were distinguished by certain insignia, which never failed to receive the respect with which similar evidences of authority are regarded in civilized countries.

It appears that the chiefs, although absolute in their powers, nevertheless took care to call around them the best informed and most respected portion of their subjects, as advisors. Thus, whenever a military expedition or other enterprise was meditated, the chief, who was called *teite*,/89/ convened a *monexica* or council, which appointed persons to assess the cost, so that it should fall equally upon the community. The councillors of the cazique were named for four months, at the end of which time they went back among the people. They were always chosen from the old men.

One of the first duties of the council was the appointment of subordinate executive officers, to act during the four months for which they were chosen, two of which were always present at the markets, to preserve the peace, and punish those who used false measures, or practiced frauds of any kind, as also those who disobeyed orders, or violated approved usages. It was also their duty to pay particular attention to strangers, and encourage them to frequent the markets or fairs.

The council houses were called *grepons*,/90/ surrounded by broad corridors called *galpóns*, beneath which the arms were kept, protected by a guard of young men. The decision of the *monexica* or council might be against the cazique, and his judgment be overruled; but he could not dissolve it, nor could it be again convened except by his orders. The war-chief was elected by the warriors to lead them, on account of his ability and bravery in battle, and had undivided command of the forces; but the civil or hereditary chief often accompanied the army, and, in case the war-chief was slain, either took his place in person or named a successor on the spot.

The spoil of battle was not divided equally among the warriors; but each one kept all he got. It was not usual to punish cowardice with death; but cowards were despoiled of their arms and driven out of the ranks in disgrace. Prisoners were much desired for sacrifices, and consequently the warriors sought rather to capture than slay their enemies. Those who acquitted themselves well in battle, or who had triumphed in hand-to-hand conflict with an enemy, took the title of *tapaliqui*,/91/ and as a mark of distinction were permitted to shave the entire head, leaving only a

88. Oviedo's *tiel*, (also *tile*—he used both spellings), carbon black from pine torches, from (N.) *tlili*, "black." (Lehmann, 1016; O&V.)

89. Sic—Oviedo spelled this *teyte*; it signified lord or cazique (n. 2), and was derived from (N.) *tecútli*, "sir." Squier unaccountably changes many spellings, not always a help for his English readers. *Monexica* (below), from N. *monechicoa*, "to collect," was a council of mayors or governors to dispense justice and maintain order in the marketplace; see also n. 102. Oviedo had *monexico*. (León-Portilla, 51, 54, 94-96; Lehmann, 1015; Radell, 38-39.)

90. Squier's text is confused here. Oviedo's word *galpón* identifies both the council house and also the high-ranking guards who protected the cazique and council members. The council house was indeed both dormitory and arsenal. "Grepon" seems to be a garbled form of *galpón*, which comes from (N.) *calpulli*, "great house." Squier's "broad corridors" may refer to (Sp.) *soportales* (porticos or arcades) that Oviedo noted in connection with the council houses. (Lehmann, 1012; Oviedo, iv 365, 377-78.)

91. Sic—Squier has transcribed the Sp. *tapaligui*, which derives from N. *tlapaliuhqui* (N. *tlapilli*, color, *hua*, he who

scalp-lock, or tuft, on the crown. This was required to be precisely half a finger in length, with a tuft in the center a little longer. The same practice also prevailed in Mexico.

Marriage among the Nicaraguan nations was a civil rite, performed by the cazique, and the ceremonies were much the same as those practiced among the Mexicans. The matches were arranged by the parents of the parties; and as soon as the bargain was concluded, two fowls and a *rula*/92/ (a kind of house-dog) were killed, some cacao prepared, and the friends and neighbors invited to the feast. This finished, the cazique led the couple into a small house, devoted to that purpose, in which a fire of resin was kindled, where, after giving them a lecture, he left them to themselves. When the fire was burned out the rite was complete. If it proved that the woman was not a virgin, she was sent back to her parents and permanently disgraced, while the man was at liberty to marry again.

The couple, after marriage, received from their parents a piece of land and certain fruit-trees which, if they died childless, reverted to their respective families. But one wife was permitted to any man except the cazique, although concubinage was practiced by those who could afford it. Bigamy was punished by exile, and by confiscation of property for the benefit of the first wife or husband, who was then at liberty to marry again. This privilege was not, however, extended to women having children.

Adultery on the part of the wife subjected her to severe flogging, and to be sent back to her family; but she still retained her effects. It liberated the husband from his marital obligations; the woman, however, could not marry again. Relationship beyond the first degree/93/ was no bar to marriage. Marriages within families, on the contrary, were encouraged as "tightening the bonds of relationship." Incest was unknown; but the man who debauched the daughter of his master or cazique was buried alive with the partner of his guilt. The man who committed rape was seized, confined, and, unless he could make reparation by large presents to the injured woman or her parents, became her or their slave. Sodomites were stoned to death.

Prostitutes were tolerated, and the price of their favors limited at ten *amands* of cacao./94/ They were accompanied by bullies (*rufianos*) who, however, did not share their gains. Establishments, or houses, of prostitution were kept publicly. On the occasion of a certain annual festival it was permitted that all the women, of whatever condition, might abandon themselves to the arms of whoever they pleased. Rigid fidelity, however, was exacted at all other times.

Parents might traffic with the persons of their daughters without subjecting themselves to punishment. Prostitution was sometimes resorted to by girls whose parents were unable to provide for them a proper marriage portion. When one of these, having by this means secured a competence, desired to withdraw from that mode of life, she procured a piece of ground whereon to build a house, and collecting her lovers, announced to them that those desirous of having her for a wife must unite and build a house, after the plan which she should furnish, and that when completed, she would select her husband from among them. The house being built and stocked, a feast was prepared, at the close of which the girl took the man of her choice by the arm and led him away, exulting to be preferred over his rivals. The rejected ones, says the chronicler, "generaly take it patiently, but occasionally one suspends himself from a tree, in order that the devil may have his part in the wedding, and is eaten for his pains."

Oviedo states that the men built the houses, cultivated the ground, hunted, and fished, while the women did the trading. If true, this was an exception to the common practice of the Indian nations, which devolved all the drudgery

has). In Mexico this title of honor was awarded to brave men; their hair was parted and wrapped in red cord with green, blue, and red feathers. Those who performed many heroic deeds received even more honors and awards, including the name *cuáchic*, "shorn man." Their heads were shaven, except for one lock of hair above the left ear, as thick as a thumb, braided with a red ribbon. One half of the head was painted blue, the other half red or yellow. (Durán, 198-99; León-Portilla, 55, 99, 100-101; Lehmann, 1014; Stone, 223.)

92. Oviedo's *xulo* (N. *xolo, xolotl*), a non-barking dog, Squier renders as *rula* (in some old typefaces *x* and *r* look similar). Oviedo had thought the dog useful in hunting, but it was solely a food source. In Mexico too the markets offered, wrote Soustelle, "the little mute hairless dogs that the Aztecs so loved to eat." (León-Portilla, 48, 88; Soustelle, 26; Sauer, 59; O&V.)

93. The Roman Catholic church recognized first cousins as a second-degree relationship, but their marriage would have been permitted here.

94. Oviedo calls cacao beans "almonds" (Sp. *almendra, amand*). The "seeds" or beans in Squier's time still had some worth as currency. See also n. 101.

upon the females. "The husband," he says, "before leaving the house, must sweep it, and kindle a fire"–duties which now, most certainly, fall upon the females./95/

In respect to their physique, they were well made and of fairer complexion than the average; and then, as now, frequently shaved the head, leaving only a circle of hair extending along the edge of the forehead, from ear to ear. They all had a custom of cleaving the under part of the tongue and of piercing their ears for the introduction of ornaments.

Like the Peruvians,/96/ the Natchez, and many other aboriginal nations, they flattened their heads. "When our children are young," said the chiefs to the Friar Bobadilla, "their heads are tender, and are then moulded into the shape which you see in us, by means of two pieces of wood, hollowed in the middle. Our gods instructed our ancestors that, by so doing, we should have a noble air, and the head be better fitted to bear burdens."

Murder, under aggravated circumstances, was punished with death; but in all cases of homicide the perpetrator gave to the next relatives of the victim a male or female slave, clothes, and other articles. Robbers had their hair cut off, and were the slaves of the injured party until complete restitution was effected.

A father might sell his own children or himself as slaves, in cases of great necessity, with the privilege of redemption. Payment of debts was rigidly required; if a man had borrowed maize or fruits, the creditor might repay himself from his debtor's fields. Any man might expatriate himself, but he could not diminish the public wealth by taking any of his property with him; he might, however, give it to his relatives.

Their dwellings seem to have been rude structures of canes, thatched with grass, identical with those now used by the poorer inhabitants. The residences of the chiefs were of the same construction, but larger and more commodious. In all the towns there were one or more public squares, or market-places, around which the temples and public edifices seem to have been built. All of these buildings, the chronicler adds, were surrounded by fruit-trees, planted so thickly and in such a manner that the square could hardly be entered.

In the center of the town of Tecoatega,/97/ as described by Oviedo, there was a "large inclosed space, the right side of which was occupied by a large house or magazine, filled with grain and provisions. Fronting this, upon the left side, was a building a hundred paces in length, the roof of which descended almost to the ground, entered by a low door, in which slept the cazique and his wives." A building open in front, and high and airy, occupied another side of the square, which was the reception-house, or court, of the cazique, where he was usually to be found, and where he was constantly surrounded by his attendants and servants. His seat was in the center of this edifice: it was a sort of bed or platform of canes, raised about three feet above the common floor, and was covered with palm-leaves and fine and brilliantly colored *petates*/98/ or mats. The cazique, in common with the people, had a sort of little bench, hollowed on the top, called a *duho*, for a pillow, which was well worked and highly polished, and sometimes used as a seat. Toward the ends of the building large mats were spread for the minor chiefs, who were the cazique's attendants./99/

Near this edifice were other smaller buildings, occupied by the domestics of the cazique's establishment; one was devoted wholly to the women who ground the maize for tortillas and tamales. There were also, in this instance, and near by, two small buildings erected as monuments over two children of the cazique who had died in infancy. Finally, upon the fourth side of the square were houses or barracks for the guards, and some fine poles covered with the heads of deer and other animals which the cazique had slain, and which were thus preserved as trophies of his skill. The guards

95. Oviedo noted that when "emancipated" by the Spaniards the men ceased their sweeping and kindling chores. These descriptions are from his Vol. iv, Book XLII, Chaps. 1-13; Palacio used them 50 years later. (Radell, 39-40.)

96. See n. 67. The chiefs' reason for flattening the head (below) seems naive: the nobility did not bear such physical burdens whatever the physiognomical implementation. For Bobadilla (below) see n. 109.

97. Tecoatega or Tecoateca was probably Tecoatlán originally. (Lehmann, 1014-15).

98. The *petate* (N. *petlatl*) was a mat woven usually from palm, reed, or rushes; it was universally a bed for sleeping and the seat of an official. Oviedo elsewhere (Book VI, Chap. 2) described the ceremonial *duhos* (below) with admiration as "some small wooden benches, very well worked of fine wood and with many figures both in relief and depressed, engraved and sculptured thereon, and these benches or low seats they call a *duho*." Most were made of ebony and highly esteemed; Kidder has observed that, like the hammock, the *duho* was probably a South American invention. (Soustelle, 122; O&V; Sauer, 60; Kidder, 445; Stone, 217.)

99. See Oviedo's plan of the cazique's plaza, p. 41.

were kept on duty day and night, relieving each other at regular intervals, and watching jealously over the person of the chief.

The caziques affected great state, and carried their exclusion so far as to receive messages from other chiefs only through officers delegated for that purpose. Oviedo illustrates their etiquette by an incident which befell himself,/100/ when he visited the chief of Tecoatega, which he did soon after his arrival in the country, in company with the governor's chaplain. The chief, he says, neither spoke to him nor deigned to look at him until he was informed that he was not only attached to the household of the emperor, but was a relative of the governor. The chief then laid aside his gravity and asked and answered questions with much spirit, "showing clearly that he was a man of talent." He nevertheless sent one of his attendants to question the servants of the party, to ascertain if what they had told him was true.

Cacao,/101/ or rather the seeds of the cacao, here, as in many other parts of tropical America, answered the chief purpose of currency, when the transaction between buyer and seller was not simple barter. There were fixed market days; but by a singular rule the privilege of trading was confined to the women, and to boys not yet arrived at puberty. No man was allowed to enter, or even to look into the *tianguez*,/102/ or market. The people of friendly villages might traffic with each other, and were freely admitted into each other's markets. All articles of production—metals, woods, fruits, and vegetables, as well as all varieties of manufactures—were exposed for sale in the *tianguez*.

They were very industrious in their habits, and skillful workers in gold/103/ and copper, and in cotton and other fabrics of *pita*, or agave. They cultivated cotton extensively, and worked it curiously, probably in the very manner still practiced, and which has already been described. Of this their clothing is made:

The men wore a sort of doublet/104/ without sleeves, and a belt which, after passing around the body, was carried between the legs and fastened behind. The women had a *nagua* hanging from the girdle as low as the knees. Those of the better orders had them falling as low as the ankle and also wore a handkerchief covering their breasts. Both sexes wore sandals made of deer skins and called *cutares*, which were fastened by a cotton cord passing between the toes and around the heel.

100. Here Squier seems to confuse Oviedo with Bobadilla, who could indeed have been the "governor's chaplain." But Bobadilla was related to the governor (see n. 109), not Oviedo. If both men attended this event historians have not so acknowledged it.

101. Mexican nobility enjoyed cacao in a variety of foods. Because it grows only in distant tropical environments, the Aztecs apparently did not concern themselves with its worship to insure good harvests.

Among the Maya, Landa noted, cacao growers celebrated a festival to Ek Chuah in the fifteenth month of Muan. Roys thought the name (M. *ek*, black, *chua*, calabash) probably refers to the color and shape of the ripe cacao pod. Ek Chuah was the god of merchants and travelers, largely because the bean was used as money.

Landa said the Yucatán growers sacrificed a cacao-colored dog, burned incense, and rendered other offerings. Traveling Aztec merchants, however, recognized the god Yacatecutli ("He who goes first") who was worshiped—with no cacao association—in the tenth month, Xocotl Huetzi. See also n. 134.

(Landa, 90, 107, 164; Durán, 204, 242; León-Portilla, 57.)

102. *Tianguez, tiangues* (N. *tianquiztli*), market; *tianquizpán tlayacaque*, supervisors or guardians who brought market disputes to nearby judges for resolution; see n. 89. In prehispanic Mexico a god of markets and fairs was mounted on a *momoztli*, a block or shrine at the marketplace decorated with carvings and flowers. One of its duties, said Durán, was to "threaten terrible ills and evil omens and auguries to the neighboring villages which did not attend. . . ." Except for Mixcoa (n. 123), Oviedo does not report a market god in Nicaragua. (Durán, 273-74, 476; León-Portilla, 50, 96; Lehmann, 1015; Soustelle, 25-28.)

103. Gold and copper were not plentiful in Central America above Panama. The copper of the canoe party (n. 107) probably came from Michoacan, said Sauer, although in Honduras natives also reported its occurrence. For *pita*, agave, see n. 133. (Sauer, 129, 137.)

104. The doublet or jacket without sleeves was the (N.) *xicolli*; the belt was the *maxtli, maxtlatl*, a loincloth. For *nagua* (below) see n. 12. Regarding *cutares* (below): Squier later has *cutara* (n. 142); Oviedo elsewhere uses *gutara*. The word came from Cuba. (Soustelle, 131-34, 138; Vaillant, 74, 139; O&V.)

Their personal ornaments were chiefly of gold and pearls. The people of Nicoya,/105/ which Oviedo expressly tells us were Chorotegans, pierced their lower lips and introduced "round pieces of white bone," and sometimes "a button of gold." The women of this section the chronicler specially commends, on account of their symmetry of figure and beauty of feature.

Their arms were identical with those used by the Mexicans, and consisted of lances and arrows pointed with flint, copper, or the bones of fishes, and a species of sword called in Mexico *mahquahuitl,*/106/ which was a tough piece of wood, with blades of obsidian set on either edge, and wielded with both hands, constituting a formidable weapon. For defense they used shields of wood, covered with hide and ornamented with feathers which, by their color and the figures they formed, signified the rank and position of the bearer.

They also had quilted jackets/107/ and short breeches covering the thighs, made of cotton, which an arrow penetrated with difficulty and which the Spaniards found to be so effective for defense that they adopted them for themselves. The accompanying cut of a soldier's dress is copied from a Mexican manuscript. The letter *a* indicates the feather head-dress; *c*, a plate of metal covering part of the face, and *d*, the cotton-quilted armor. They did not poison their weapons.

SOLDIER'S DRESS, FROM A MEXICAN MANUSCRIPT.

Gold seems to have been used only for ornamental purposes and for making little idols to be worshiped in their houses and temples. They had among them certain manuscripts which the Spaniards called "books" and which seem to have been identical with those possessed by the Mexicans. They were painted "in black and red colors, on parchment made from the skins of deer, and were a hand's breadth or upwards in width, and ten or twelve yards long, and folded like a screen." "Though these characters," continues Oviedo, "were neither letters nor figures, they were not without their meaning."/108/

105. In describing its people Squier has used Niquirans for Nicaráos (n. 23); here he introduces their territory as Nicoya—presumably derived from the name of the inhabitants, reflected by their leader's use of it.

106. Sic—also N. *macuahuitl.* Sauer has pointed out that the (Sp.) word *macana* for this weapon originated in the Caribbean islands, where its use as an agricultural tool (somewhat like a machete) was more common. (Valliant, 66, 210, 221; Sauer, 52.)

107. The quilted jacket of the Aztec warrior was the *ichcahuipilli* (N. *ichca*, cotton, *huipilli*, blouse), made of wadded cotton soaked in brine.

Ferdinand Columbus' description of a Maya canoe party earlier furnished Oviedo some details of long-distance trade and merchandise. On Guanaja, an island on the north coast of Honduras, the Admiral encountered a 25-man dugout loaded with wares:

> He then ordered that there should be taken from the canoe whatever appeared to be most attractive and valuable, such as cloths and sleeveless shirts of cotton that had been worked and dyed in different colors and designs, also pantaloons of the same workmanship with which they cover their private parts, also cloth in which the Indian women of the canoe were dressed. . . . Also long swords of wood with a groove along each edge, wherein stone knives were set by means of fiber and pitch, cutting like steel when used on naked people; also hatchets to cut wood, like those of stone used by other Indians, save for the fact that these were of good copper, of which metal they also had bells and crucibles for smelting. . . .

Although Columbus did not recognize its implications, the merchant canoe suggested heavy trade between central Mexico and the Gulf of Honduras. Such Mexican traders later served as interpreters and guides in subsequent conquests, giving the Spaniards Nahuatl names even for non-Aztec areas.
(Sauer, 128-29; Soustelle, 210; Vaillant, 66, 210.)

108. Means has pointed out that calendrical lore and the hieroglyphics that necessarily conveyed it went no further south than Nicaragua. Both the calendar and a writing system never reached South America. (Philip A. Means, "The Philosophic Interrelationship between Middle America and Andean Regions." Hay et al., 434.)

RELIGION, ETC.

As we have seen, it was asserted by Oviedo that while they differed widely in their habits and modes of life, the inhabitants of Nicaragua nevertheless agreed substantially in their religion. This appears to have been the same—or very nearly the same—with that of Mexico; and among the Niquirans the names of the gods, as well as the rites with which they were worshiped, including the practice of human sacrifices, were identical with those of the Aztecs and their neighbors in the valley of Anahuac. The nature of their beliefs, as also the prescriptions of their ritual, appear very clearly from the records preserved by Oviedo.

Among these is a transcript of the proceedings of a commission, of which the Fray Francisco de Bobadilla,/109/ Provincial of the Order of Mercy, was the head, delegated by Pedro Arias de Avila, Governor of Nicaragua, in 1528, to procure an exact account of the condition of the Indians, to ascertain the nature of their religion, and to discover how far they had been affected by the introduction of Christianity. It was on the 28th of September of the same year that Bobadilla arrived in the province of Niquira and commenced his investigation.

The first who appeared before him was a chief named Chichoyatona,/110/ whom Bobadilla piously proceeded to baptize, naming him Alonzo de Herrera. He then inquired of him if he knew there was a God who had created man, the world, and all things. But Chichoyatona either did not know, or else did not care to answer questions, and the friar got nothing from him. He next tried an old man named Cipat, but he replied to the same question that he neither knew nor cared, and was accordingly dismissed. It is not, however, to be supposed that Cipat was really so ignorant; for the Indians of Nicaragua, in common with those of every part of the continent, were extremely jealous of all things relating to their religion.

Bobadilla, no wise discouraged, tried another chief, named Mizeztoy,/111/ and this time with better success. Mizeztoy stated that he was a Christian; that is to say, had had water poured on his head by a priest, but had really quite forgot what name had been bestowed on him. The result of his examination is given by the chronicler as follows:

> Friar: Do you know who made heaven and earth?
> Indian: My parents told me, when I was a child, that it was *Famagostad*/112/ and *Zipaltonal*, the first male and the second female.

109. Fray Bobadilla was related to Pedrarias (n. 16), whose daughter was doña Isabel Bobadilla, and lived for a time with the governor in Panama. It is generally supposed that Oviedo met Bobadilla either in Nicaragua or in Spain; Oviedo (see n. 100) suggests that they met in Nicaragua. Although Bobadilla himself on one occasion—a nine-day period—baptized 43,000 Indians, he knew such mass conversions had no permanence. He later became *provincial* (director) of a Mercedarian chapter in Peru. The Order of Our Lady of Mercy, founded in the thirteenth century, was very active in Central America. (Squier, ii 361; León-Portilla, 20, 22; Oviedo, v 428.)

110. Sic—Squier transcribed Oviedo's Chicoyatónal, which León-Portilla believed to be Chicueiatónal originally. For Herrera see n. 80. Cipat (below) is from Sp. *çípat*, N. *cipacti* (crocodile—see n. 110). (Lehmann, 1011; León-Portilla, 37.)

111. Sic—Squier took this form from Ternaux-Compans; Oviedo had Misésboy. León-Portilla found it impossible to identify the Nahuatl (Lehmann had earlier suggested *miz-tli*, "puma blood"). (León-Portilla, 37; Lehmann, 1012.)

112. "Famagostad" is Squier's most puzzling alteration of the original, Tamagástad; the "F" appears to be a misreading—perhaps of a battered letter "T." The Nicaraguan Tamagástad itself was a corruption of (N.) *tlamacázcatl* (also *tlamacázqui*—see n. 124). León-Portilla said it signified a "provider or giver of gifts," pointing out that in Mexico it was frequently used to describe both priests and the highest gods of all. Soustelle explained:

> When he was between twenty and twenty-two years old ... //the novice// became a *tlamacazqui*, a priest, and from then onwards he could assume this venerated title, which was in fact the attribute of Quetzalcoatl, god, king and high-priest of the legendary Tula. It was also the title given to Tlaloc, the ancient god of rain and fecundity, to the lesser divinities who attended him, and to the splendid, beneficent young god of music and dancing //Piltzintecuhtli//. To be entitled *tlamacazqui* was, to some degree, to be already the equal of a god. ...

Zipaltonal (Oviedo's Cipattóral) in Mexico was Cipactónal (from N. *cipactli*, serpent, crocodile); "Cipac-tónal" referred more specifically to a person or god whose *tonalli* (calendar day sign) was Cipactli, land monster or crocodile,

F.: What are they, men or animals?

I.: I do not know; my parents never saw them, nor do I know whether they dwell in the air or elsewhere.

F.: Who created man, and all things?

I.: As I have already said, Famagostad and Zipaltonal, a younger named Ecalchot,/113/ a *guegue*, and little Ciagat.

F.: Where are they?

I.: I do not know, except that they are our great gods, whom we call *teotes*./114/

F.: Have they parents or ancestors?

I.: No; for they are gods.

F.: Do the teotes eat?

I.: I do not know; but when we make war, we do so that they may eat the blood of our enemies whom we have slain or taken prisoners. We scatter the blood on all sides, in order that the teotes may make sure of it; for we know not on which side they dwell, nor even that they do really consume it.

F.: Do you know, or have you even heard, that the world has been destroyed since the creation?

I.: I have heard our fathers say that it was destroyed by water,/115/ a very long time ago.

F.: Were all men drowned?

I.: I do not know; but the teotes rebuilt the world, and placed upon it men and animals again.

F.: How did the teotes escape? upon a mountain or in a canoe?

I.: They are gods—how could they drown?

F.: Were all animals and the birds drowned?

I.: Those now existing were created anew by the teotes, as well as men and all things.

F.: Are all the Indians acquainted with what you have just told me?

I.: The priests of the temples and the caziques know it.

F.: By whom are the teotes served?

I.: The old men say that those who are slain in battle serve the teotes, and that those who die in the natural way go under the earth.

F.: Which is most honorable, to go under the earth, or to serve the teotes?

I.: By far, to serve the teotes, because we shall then meet with our fathers.

the first day of the month. Cipactónal was the feminine god accompanying Oxomoco (n. 113), inventors together of the calendar, as well as a race of beings who preceded humans. Davies:

> Oxomoco and Cipactonal are a fairly familiar pair of sorcerers or magicians. They occur in Quiche legends //e.g. Popol Vuh// as Xpiyacoc and Xmucane and among Nahua speakers of Nicaragua as Tamagastad and Cipattonal. . . .

The Quiché "divine grandparents," Xpiyacac and Xmucane, appear to be older concepts than the other gods, the origin of their names lost in the lexicon.

(Tedlock, 369-70; León-Portilla, 43, 61, 63; Durán, 399, 406, 469; Davies, 94; O&V; Soustelle, 51.)

113. Ecalchot (sic—Oviedo's Chalchitgüegüe) was a corruption of (N.) Chalchiuhtlicue ("She who has a skirt of gems"), the wife or female companion of Tlaloc. She was the goddess of fresh water, fertility, and abundance. Ciagat (sic—Oviedo's Chicoçiágat) represents the calendrical name of a god, Chicoace Acatl, "Six Cane." "Little" Ciagat was Ternaux-Compans' attempt to read Oviedo's "chico" as "petit."

Squier curiously omits another deity mentioned by Mizeztoy: Oxomogo or Oxomoco, who was Cipactónal's companion (n. 112). Oxomoco evidently derives from N. *amoxoaque*, "//wise// men who were versed in the ancient painted documents," according to Sahagún (in Davies). Sahagún named Oxomoco and Cipactónal as elders who remained at Teotihuacan when it collapsed. Apparently the priestly title *tamagástad* was more persistent, obscuring the fact that the priest was indeed named Oxomoco.

(Davies, 113; León-Portilla, 43, 61, 66-67; O&V; Lehmann, 1011, Durán, 221-28; Soustelle, 103.)

114. Sic—this is, according to León-Portilla, a corruption of N. *teteo*, plural of *téot*, god; León-Portilla also cited Oviedo's use of *thomaotheot* (a corruption of N. *tomactéot*, "grand god"). (León-Portilla, 43, 59, 62, 69-70.)

115. León-Portilla noted that all three natives interrogated agreed that the world had been destroyed by universal flood. It seems unlikely that they were influenced by the biblical Flood about which later Spanish priests would sermonize. (León-Portilla, 43, 59, 62, 69-70.)

I.: If the parents die, I know not what becomes of the children.

F.: Finally, what is their destiny?

I.: I know only what I have told you; and it must be true, because our fathers have told us so.

F.: But if your fathers have died in their beds, how can you meet them?

I.: Our fathers are themselves teotes.

F.: Can the teotes bring the dead to life, and if so, where are the re-awakened dead?

I.: All that I know is that infants who die before they are weaned, and before they have tasted maize, will be raised again, and return to their parents' houses, where their fathers will recognize and provide for them; whilst on the other hand, those who die at a more advanced age will never come to life again.

F.: But if the parent should die before his children come to life again, how can he recognize or provide for them?

The Fray Bobadilla next questioned the cazique Abalgoalteogan,/116/ who also bore the name of Francisco and said he was a Christian. His testimony as to the gods coincided with that of Mizeztoy, and with him he affirmed that all knowledge concerning them was perpetuated by oral tradition; that formerly the priests had conversed with the gods, but that since the arrival of the Christians the latter had withdrawn from earth; that although the teotes are of flesh, and male and female, yet they are uncreated, immortal, enjoy eternal youth, and reside in the heavens. That the earth was once destroyed by water and became a great sea; and that afterwards Famagostad and Zipaltonal descended, dispersed the waters, and recreated all things.

That of the dead, the good alone go above with the teotes, the bad to a subterranean abode named Mique-tanteot;/117/ that there is no resurrection of the body, but by the act of death "there comes forth from the mouth something which resembles the person, called *julio*, which goes to the place of the teotes. It is immortal: but the body decays for ever." The good are those "who take care of the temples, and observe the laws of friendship; the wicked are those who do differently, and they are sent under the earth."

The Fray next interrogated an old man, past sixty years of age, named Tacoteyda,/118/ who was a priest in one of the temples of Nicaragua. He concurred entirely with the others in representing Famagostad and Zipaltonal as themselves uncreated, the creators of heaven and earth, and the greatest of gods. He added that they resembled the Indians themselves, were ever young, dwelt in the heavens towards the rising of the sun, and that their aid in war or for other purposes, previously to the arrival of the Christians, was procured by addressing petitions to heaven.

Tacoteyda testified that Famagostad and Zipaltonal received to themselves, at their abiding-place in the eastern heavens, those who had lived worthily or had been slain in battle, but that all others were sent under the earth; that those who went above did not carry their bodies with them, but only *a heart*, or rather that which was the cause of life, and whose departure from the body caused death. The Fray asked him what the gods would do when all men ceased to live: to which the Indian priest replied, very frankly, that he did not know; nor did he know anything of a flood which had destroyed the world. Altogether, his examination does not appear to have been satisfactory to the Fray Bobadilla, who dismissed him, and sent for an Indian named Coyen,/119/ who was very aged, exceeding eighty years, and whose head was white as cotton wool.

He said he was a Christian, or rather that water had been poured on his head, and he had had a new name given him, which, however, he had forgotten. His testimony, in respect to the gods, confirmed what had been said by the others; they were immortal—resembled the Indians—were ever young—dwelt on high—anciently communicated with the priests

116. Sic—Squier transcribed Oviedo's Avagoalteogan, which León-Portilla thought should be Ahuacoatltecohuan. Lehmann had proposed that *tegoan* was *teguan, tequani,* "tiger," "jaguar." (Lehmann, 1009, 1015; León-Portilla, 42.)

117. Sic—Oviedo's Migtanteot; Miquetantéot (N. *mic, mique,* death) is the region of the dead—hell. Miqtantéot was also identified by the Nicaraguans as the lord of the underworld; Mictlantecuhtli and Mictlancíhuatl are also male-female underworld deities. N. *julio* (below) or *yulio* can be understood as spirit, soul, although sometimes synonymous with *yólotl,* heart. (León-Portilla, 46, 62, 69, 80; Lehmann, 1016.)

118. Sic—Squier transcribed the Sp. Taçoteyda, which León-Portilla thought was originally Tazoteuhti (Lehmann had offered *tlaço-tecutli,* "dear sir"). (León-Portilla, 44; Lehmann, 1014.)

119. Coyen is Oviedo's Coyévet; León-Portilla believed this should be Coyéhuet, N. *coy, coyotl,* coyote, *huet,* old. (León-Portilla, 37, 42, 43; Lehmann, 1014; Molina.)

in the temples, but did so no longer, and loved the blood and hearts of children, and the perfume of resins. He had heard, from his ancestors, that the world had been destroyed by water in remote times, and that none was saved, but that the gods had created the world anew. The good went on high with the teotes, the bad below the earth. The body putrified in the ground, but the principle of life, which dwelt in the heart, and which was immortal, went above.

The Fray afterwards collected thirteen Indians, priests, caziques, and others, and made various inquiries of them, which, with their answers, are given below. It should be remembered, however, that the Fray was now among the Niquirans, or people of Mexican stock. The Fray first asked them if they were the original inhabitants of the country; to which they answered that although their ancestors had been there from time immemorial they were not the true aborigines, but came originally from a distant country called Ticomega Emaguatega,/120/ which was situated towards the west, i.e. NW. They quitted because they had masters who ill-treated them.

Friar: Were these masters Indians or Christians?

Indian: Indians.

F.: What was the service which was required of your fathers?

I.: They tilled the ground, and served their masters as we now serve the Christians. Their masters overtasked, abused, and even ate them. It was fear which induced them to migrate. Their masters came from another country, and by numbers and force overcame them.

F.: What is your religion? Whom do you worship?

I.: We adore Famagostad and Zipaltonal, who are our gods.

F.: Who sends you rain and all other things?

I.: The rain is sent by Quiatéot,/121/ son of the god Home-Atelite and the goddess Home-Ateciguat. They dwell at the extremity of the world, where the sun goes.

F.: Have they ever lived on earth?

I.: No.

F.: From whence do they come?

I.: We know not.

F.: Who made the heavens and earth, and all things else?

I.: Famagostad and Zipaltonal.

120. Sic—Oviedo gave the country of origin as Ticomega é //and// Maguatega. Lehmann accepted Torquemada's assertion that the Nicaraguans were a branch of Pipils who had migrated south; based on their dialect, called Nahuat (the *tl* phoneme had disappeared), Lehmann estimated that the movement occurred about 1000 A.D. rather than Torquemada's 800. Lehmann further claimed he had found a Cholulá document referring to Ticomega and Maguatega as local toponyms.

The more probable forms for these sites were Ticoman or Ticomatlán and Miahuatlán. There is, however, no explanation as to why these particular place names were so venerated, especially since the Olmec subjugation (n. 59) occurred in Chiapas.

Lothrop also perceived that designs on Nicaraguan pottery had similarities to those of the Cholulá region, and dated the movement to the end of the eleventh century. Local sculptures, including ballgame yokes and *hachas*, may also have been carried to Chiapas, Verapaz, and highland Guatemala at this time by Pipil migrants.

(León-Portilla, 30; Davies, 119-20; Lothrop 1940, 420; Lehmann, 1015-16.)

121. Quiatéot corresponds to the classic Mexican (N.) Quiahtéotl, who was also a rain god (Quiahuitl, "rainstorm," was a month name). León-Portilla noted that these interviewed Nicaraguans never speak of Tlaloc, the principal Mexican god of rain, although Mizetoy's reference to babies who die in infancy returning to their parents probably represents a vestige of Tlaloc's paradisical "warm gardens" where the dead find repose.

Home-Atelite (sic—Oviedo had Omeyateite) and Home-Ateciguat (sic—Omeyatecígoat) refer to the supreme male and female Mexican divinities, Ometecuhtli (N. *ome*, dual, *tecuhtli*, lord) and Omecíhuatl (*cíhuatl*, lady), who ruled over the heavens. Another name for them was Ometéotl, the dual god, as well as Teteuh innan and Teteuh intah, mother and father of the gods.

León-Portilla rendered the response (below), "what relates to water," as "what relates to the god of water."

(Durán, 154-55, 403; Soustelle, 96, 98, 107, 116, 202; León-Portilla, 43, 62, 67-68, 84; Padden, 28; O&V; Lehmann, 1014.)

F.: Did they make the father and mother of Quiatéot?

I.: No; what relates to water is an entirely different thing, but we know very little of the matter.

F.: Has Quiatéot a wife?

I.: No.

F.: Who serve him?

I.: We think he ought to have servants, but we know not who they are.

F.: What does he eat?

I.: What we do; for our food has come from the gods.

F.: Which do you regard as the most powerful, the father, mother, or son?

I.: They are equal to one another.

F.: When do you ask for rain, and what do you do to obtain it?

I.: We go to the temple dedicated to him, and sacrifice some young children. After having cut off their heads, we sprinkle the blood on the images and stone idols in the house of prayer consecrated to our gods, and which in our language is called *teobat.*/122/

F.: What do you do with the bodies of the sacrificed?

I.: Those of the children we bury; those of the men are eaten by the caziques and chiefs, but not by the rest of the people.

F.: When this is done, does the god send you rain?

I.: Sometimes he does, but sometimes not.

F.: Why do you go to the temples, and what do you say and do there?

I.: The temples are to us what the churches are to Christians; there are our gods, and there we burn perfumes in their honor; we ask of them health if we are sick; rain if it is needed, for we are poor, and if the earth should be parched we can have no fruits—in short, we ask of them all things of which we stand in need. The principal cazique enters the temple and prays in the name of all; the rest of the Indians do not enter. The cazique remains there for prayer an entire year, and during that time never leaves the temple. When he comes forth, a great festival is celebrated in his honor, with dancing and feasting. His nostrils are then pierced, to show that he has been pontiff of the temple, which is esteemed to be the greatest of honors. Another chief is then sought to take his place, so that there may always be one in the temple. As to those temples, which are only a kind of oratorio, anyone can place in them one of his children; and anyone who desires may enter, provided he is unmarried, on condition of not having connection with any woman for an entire year—that is to say, until the caziques and priests who are in the temple shall have come out.

F.: Are married persons who are willing to quit their wives and go into the temples suffered to do so?

I.: Yes. But at the expiration of the year they must return to their wives, and if caziques, resume their government.

F.: How are they provided with food?

I.: It is brought to them by children from the house of the priests; and during all the time they are in the temple no one can enter it beyond the vestibule, except those young persons who carry provisions.

F.: While in the temple do they converse with the gods?

I.: For a long time our gods have not visited or conversed with us. If our ancestors may be believed, they were once in the habit of doing so. All that we know is that the person charged with praying to the gods asks of them all things needful.

F.: In time of war, do they come forth from the temple?

I.: No. The vestibule of the temple is very convenient for meeting.

F.: Who clean and sweep the temples?

I.: Young boys only; married or old men take no part in the matter.

F.: Have you, during the year, any prescribed days of general attendance at the temple?

I.: We have twenty-one festival days for amusement, drinking, and dancing around the court, but no one is permitted to enter the temple.

---

122. *Teobat* is Squier's form for Oviedo's *teoba,* "house of oration," probably from (N.) *teopán,* temple. In Mexico the word *teocalli* (*teo,* god, *calli,* house) designated a structure of similar purpose, but apparently more formal, more grand. (Soustelle, 4, 15; Vaillant, 137-38; Lehmann, 1015.)

F.: Do the women take any part in collecting the straw, bringing wood, or anything else which may be of use either in building or repairing the temple?

I.: The women can take no part in anything which concerns the temple, and are never admitted within it.

F.: Since you sometimes sacrifice women, do you not violate the law which forbids them from entering the temple?

I.: When women are sacrificed in the temples or principal houses of prayer, they are first put to death in the court; but it is allowable to introduce them into the ordinary temples.

F.: What do you do with the blood of those who are sacrificed in the courts of the principal temples?

I.: It is brought into the temple, and the priest sprinkles it on the idols with his hands.

F.: What do you do with the body?

I.: It is eaten; except the bodies of females, which are not touched. When the victim is a man, the priest has his share.

F.: Are those who are sacrificed voluntary victims: are they selected by lot? or is it a punishment inflicted upon them?

I.: They are slaves, or prisoners of war.

F.: As you esteem your gods so much, how can you sacrifice persons of infamous condition to them?

I.: Our ancestors did so, and we do likewise.

F.: Do you make any other offerings in your temples?

I.: Everyone brings such offerings as he pleases, such as fowls, maize, fish, fruits, etc. They are carried to the temple by the young people.

F.: Who eats these offerings?

I.: The priest of the temple; and if any remains, it is eaten by the boys.

F.: Are the provisions cooked before being carried to the temples?

I.: Always.

F.: Does anyone taste of these offerings before the priest?

I.: No one presumes to touch or taste of them before him; for this is considered one of the most important regulations of the temple.

F.: Why do you make a self-sacrifice by cutting the tongue?

I.: We always do this before we purchase, sell, or conclude a bargain, because we believe it will bring us a fortunate result. The god we invoke on such occasions is named Mixcoa./123/

F.: Who is your god Mixcoa?

I.: Carved stones, which we invoke in his honor.

F.: How do you know this god will aid your bargains?

I.: Because when we invoke him we make good bargains.

F.: Has Nicaragua ever been visited by any nation other than the Spaniards, who might have taught you all these ceremonies, ordered you to pour water on your heads, or to cut off the foreskin? and did you know that the Christians were on the eve of coming to your country?

I.: We know nothing of all this; but since you have come among us, you have told us it was good to pour water on the head, and to be baptized.

F.: What is it that is cleansed by pouring water on the head?

I.: The heart.

F.: How do you know that the heart is cleansed?

I.: We only know that it purifies us; it is the duty of your priests to explain how.

F.: At your death how do you dispose of your property, and what precautions do you take for another life?

I.: When we die, we recommend our children and property to our survivors, that they may not perish but be

123. Sic—Mixcóatl ("Cloud serpent") in the Aztec pantheon was another name for Camaxtli, god of the hunt. As a human ancestor he had earlier guided northern Mexican Nahuatl-speaking "Chichimecs," some of whom migrated by boat to Nicaragua a century or so before the Spaniards arrived. The Nicaraguan Mixcoa, as patron of business transactions, apparently was associated with "carved stones" in a manner similar to the Maya divining stones, *am*, cast by sorcerers to make decisions. See also Ek Chuah (n. 101). (Landa, 130, 154, 155; León-Portilla, 27, 45, 62, 68; Durán, 146-47; Lehmann, 1012.)

taken care of after we are dead. He who lives a good life after death goes on high among the teotes; if a bad one, below the earth.

F.: Who are your gods?

I.: Famagostad and Zipaltonal; and when we go to them they say, "here come our children!"

F.: Why do you break the idols upon your tombs?

I.: In order that they may think of us for twenty or thirty days; after that they forget us.

F.: Why, at the death of any one of you, do you paint yourselves with red paints, decorate yourselves with plumes, singing, playing on instruments, and celebrating festivals?

I.: We do nothing of the kind. When our children die, we envelope them in cotton cloth, and bury them before our doors. We leave all our property to our children, who are our heirs, if legitimate; that is to say, the children of a husband and wife and born in the house; but they are not our heirs if born of other women, or out of the house; for those only are legitimate who are born in the house. If we die without children, all we possess is buried with us.

F.: What are your funeral ceremonies?

I.: Upon the death of a chief or cazique, a large quantity of cotton cloth, shirts, cloaks, plumes, hunting horns, and all sorts of articles belonging to the dead—a portion of each kind—is burned with the body, together with all the gold he possessed. Afterwards all the ashes are gathered together, placed in an earthen vase, and buried before the house of the deceased.

F.: Why do you not bury them in your temples?

I.: Because it is not customary.

F.: Do you place provisions in the vase?

I.: At the time of burning, a little maize is placed in a calabash, by the side of the dead body, and burned with it.

F.: The heart, *julio*, or soul, does it die with the body?

I.: If the deceased has lived well, the *julio* goes on high with the gods; if not, it perishes with the body, and is no more.

F.: Do the Indians see anything at the moment of dying?

I.: They have visions of persons, lizards, serpents, and many things which fill them with fear. They know thereby that they must die. The objects which they see do not speak, but strive to frighten them. Sometimes the dead return to this world, and appear to the living for the same object.

F.: Do not the crosses placed above the dead, by the Christians, protect them?

I.: Much; for since this practice of the Christians was introduced, we have no more visions.

F.: Who taught you to give your idols the form which they have?

I.: Our fathers left us idols of stone, and from them, as models, have we made those in our houses.

F.: Why do you have them in your houses?

I.: That we may easily invoke them when necessary.

F.: Do you sacrifice to the idols in your houses?

I.: No.

F.: Before your temples stand earthen huts of a circular form, and terminating in a point; they resemble a sheaf of grain in appearance; the summit is reached by a stairway through the middle of the hut: what is the name of these huts, and what is their use?

I.: Their name is *tezarit*; the priest of the temple, whose name is *Tamagoz*, /124/ ascends to the summit of the hut, and there makes the sacrifices of the victims, sprinkling their blood on the stone idols.

The Fray Bobadilla afterwards continued his inquiries in respect to other matters, with what results will be seen

---

124. Sic—Oviedo transcribed this *tamagast, tamacastoval* (plural?); it was necessarily derived, according to Lehmann, from *tamachas, tamazcati,* "little angels," "spirits," or "genies." Squier suggests "Tamagoz" was a proper name, but (recognizing a lost "l") León-Portilla defined the word as a priest, "dedicated to making sacrifices and teaching the doctrine of their gods. To him also belong a knowledge of the calendar and the organization of religious festivals." In Mexico the corresponding *tlamacazqui* (N. *tlamacaz,* puberty; perfect man; priest), according to León-Portilla, means "makers of offerings," referring to the duty of offering incense (see n. 112). For *tezarit* (above) see n. 127. (León-Portilla, 54, 59, 62, 70, 95, 97; Durán, 113, 119; Soustelle, 51; Lehmann, 1014.)

elsewhere. He ascertained that the god of hunger was called Vizteot,/125/ and the god of the air, Chiquinau or Hecact, which last was probably intended for Ehecatl, the Mexican name for air or wind. He also ascertained the names of the days of their months, which entirely coincided with those of Mexico, as also many interesting facts connected with their religious ceremonies.

They affirmed that they had twenty-one principal festivals each year, on which occasions no work was done, but the entire people surrendered themselves to rejoicing and the observance of the prescribed rites. During these periods they abstained from all connection with their wives; the females sleeping within the houses, and the males without. This abstinence was deemed most essential, and any infraction, it was supposed, would be summarily punished by the gods. It does not appear that fasting was enjoined on any occasion.

The Spaniards were very much surprised, both here and in Mexico, at finding a well established rite, corresponding entirely with that of confession as it existed in the Catholic Church. The confession was not, however, made to the priests but to certain old men, who always maintained the strictest reserve in respect to what was communicated to them. The penances were imposed for the benefit of the temple. These old men were chosen by the council and wore a calabash suspended from their necks as a mark of dignity. It was requisite that they should be unmarried, and distinguished for their virtues. Neglect of religious ceremonies and blasphemy of the gods were regarded as offences requiring early confession and absolution, lest they should entail sickness or death on the offender. No person was required to confess himself, however, until after he had attained the age of puberty.

They seem to have had a great variety of superstitious notions, corresponding generally with those prevailing among the other Indian nations, both to the northward and southward. Among these was the practice of throwing sticks or grass upon certain stones at the road side, in passing; by which they thought they would be less subjected to hunger and fatigue. They had also a superstition, something like that of the "evil eye" among the Arabs and some other Oriental nations. They supposed there were persons whose looks were mortal, and whose eyes were fatal to children. They had also a great fear of sorcerers, whom they called *texoxes.*/126/

Oviedo has not described the temples to which he so frequently refers, but Cerezeda informs us that they were built of timber and thatched; but large, with many low, dark, inner chapels. These, it seems, were surrounded by large courts, beyond which none except the priests and the cazique during his year's novitiate dared to pass. Besides these, there were what the Indians called *tezarit,*/127/ oratorios, or "high places," which stood before or around the temples, and which Oviedo describes as being conical or pyramidal in shape, ascended by steps. Upon these the human victims were sacrificed.

Within view of their temples //says Cerezeda, who is more explicit,// there were diverse bases or pillars like pulpits, erected in the fields, of unburned brick and a certain kind of clammy earth called bitumen, which are

125. Sic—Squier transcribed the Sp. Bistéot, from N. Apizteut (*apiztli*, hunger, *teotl*, god), which also meant "glutton," god of hunger. Oviedo had originally found no Aztec god equivalent to Bistéot (there is no "b" in Nahuatl). To thwart the Aztec god of famine, Apizteotl, offerings of food were made at the temples, and, after eating, all went to a river or spring to wash themselves and their agricultural tools. León-Portilla wondered if this god was an allusion to "*el dios gordo*," the fat god, known archaeologically.

"Chiquinau or Hecact" (sic) is Squier's transcription of Chiquináut Hécat, the Nicaraguan god of the air. Like Squier, León-Portilla associated this with Ehécatl, whose Aztec references are abundant. Ehécatl ("Wind") was a day of the Aztec week. "Chicnahui Ehécatl," "Nine Wind" appears in the Codex Telleriano-Remesis; it is Quetzalcoatl's birthday. "A feast to the Air," Durán wrote, celebrated Ehécatl as one of Quetzalcoatl's names, god of merchants and jewelers. At a great feast in Huey Tecuilhuitl, the eighth month, a man was sacrificed to him. (Durán, 262-63, 432, 473; O&V; León-Portilla, 52, 62, 69, 70; Lehmann, 1010, 1011.)

126. Oviedo said the sorcerers were male and female, and believed capable of turning into crocodiles, dogs, tigers, or any animal they wished. León-Portilla found similar references to *texoxqui* (from N. *xoxa*, to bewitch, curse) in the Mexican valley. (León-Portilla, 59, 102; Lehmann, 1015.)

127. *Tezarit* reflects Squier's preference for Ternaux-Compans' spelling. Oviedo's word was *tescuit*, which Lehmann without explanation traced to N. *texcalhuia*, to throw down, i.e. "heap," "mound." There seem to be no extant examples of the architectural feature it describes. (León-Portilla, 54; Lehmann, 1015; O&V.)

from eight to fifteen steps in height. The summit is flat, and varies in size, according to the purposes for which it is designed. Some are broad enough to hold ten men.

In the middle of this space standeth a stone, higher than the rest, equalling a man's body in length; and this accursed stone is the altar of their miserable sacrifices. Upon the appointed day of sacrifice, the king ascendeth another of these altars, whence he may view the ceremony, and the people gather about; when the priest, in full view of all, from this eminent place, performeth the office of preacher, and shaking a sharp knife of stone which he holds in his hand, proclaims that a sacrifice is to be made, and also whether it is to be a prisoner or one who is a slave, or has been kept from infancy for this purpose. For every chief maintains certain persons for sacrifice who are fed daintily, and so far from being sad and sorrowful in anticipation of their fate, are persuaded that, by this kind of death, they shall be turned into gods and heavenly creatures. They are reverently received wherever they go, and whatever they ask is given to them.

Those to be sacrificed are stretched out flat on the stone whereof I have spoken, and the priest, cutting open the breast, plucks out the heart, wherewith he anoints the mouths of the idols. The body is then cut in pieces, and distributed among the priests, nobility, and the people. But the head is hung, as a trophy, upon the branches of certain small trees which are preserved for that purpose near the place of sacrifice./128/ The parts which are distributed they partly bury before their doors, but the rest they burn, leaving the ashes in the field of sacrifice.

According to Herrera, the high-places above described stood within the courts of the temples. He also informs us that the sacrifices were frequently attended by ceremonies in which all the people joined—by dances, penances, and processions. In these processions the priests wore cotton surplices, sometimes short, and sometimes long, hanging to the ground and heavily fringed. They also carried little bags of powdered herbs. The people followed, each person bearing a little flag, "with the representation of the idol which he most venerated," and carrying also their weapons of war:

Their standard //quaintly observes the chronicler// was the picture of the devil set on a spear, and carried by the eldest priest, the religious men singing the while, to the place of worship. The ground was then covered with carpets, and strewn with flowers. When the standard halted, the singing ceased, and all commenced praying. At a signal from the chief priest they punctured various parts of their bodies, and receiving the blood on paper, rubbed it on the face of the idol; and in the meantime the youths skirmished and danced in honor of the festival. The wounds were cured with the powder and herbs carried by the priests. . . . The ceremonies ended, //says Cerezeda,// the priests bow down to the spear a little, at which time the priests first, and then the nobles, and lastly the people, whisper into the ear of the idol, and everyone uttereth the tempestuous outrage of his mind, and bending the head to one shoulder, with reverent trembling and mumbling, they humbly beseech that, luckily and happily, he would favor their desires.

There was another rite, practiced at certain times, connected with a worship that prevailed to a greater extent in America than has generally been supposed, and which reveals to us the rationale of many remarkable observances otherwise inexplicable. It consisted in sprinkling blood, drawn from the organs of generation, upon maize, which was afterwards distributed and eaten with great solemnity./129/ This scenical rite, under one form or another, may be traced through the rituals of all the semi-civilized nations of America, in strict parallelism with certain phallic rites of the Hindus, and of those other numerous nations of the old world which were devoted to a similar primitive religion.

128. Stone suggested the practice of mounting heads may have developed from a hunting ritual displaying animal skulls. The resemblance of the human head to the spherical calabash (n. 9) and other large tree-grown pods (papaya, cacao) apparently encouraged the practice of hanging trophy heads from tree branches. The Mexican *tzompantli* or skull rack was simply a later, more efficient structure; Kidder believed the collection and display of skulls actually emanated from Peru. The Popol Vuh has brilliantly incorporated the practice into its narrative, with Hun-hunahpu's head, when so hung, continuing to function. (Durán, 79; Stone, 231; Kidder, 447-48; Tedlock.)

129. Squier shortly quotes Oviedo on this ritual, but in neither place does he reveal the "many remarkable observances otherwise inexplicable."

FESTIVALS

The Nicaraguans, besides their strictly sacred festivals, also had some others of a semi-religious nature, instituted in acknowledgment of successful harvests, which they call a *mitole*./130/ Oviedo was present at one of these that took place at Tecoatega belonging to a chief called Ageiteite,/131/ "the Old," who was one of the most powerful caziques of the country, having no less than twenty thousand subjects, of whom six thousand were warriors. He described it as follows:

The cacao harvest had just been finished; and the *mitole* was celebrated in the following manner:

Sixty men, with whom were mingled women and children, executed a dance. Their heads were adorned with superb bunches of feathers; and though completely naked, the whole body was so painted as to appear like clothing, and with so much art, that anyone would consider them as well clothed as the German Guard. This painting was done with cotton of various colors, spun and cut very fine, like the down from cloth, and stuck on the body. Some of them wore plumed masks. They danced in couples around the square; the distance between each of the sets being two or three paces. A pole about forty-eight hands high/132/ had been erected in the middle of the square, on the top of which was seated a well painted idol, representing, as they told me, the god Cacaguat, or "Cacao." Around this mast were placed four stakes, in the form of a square. At the extremity was attached a cord of linen, or of a kind of aloe-wood,/133/ *pité*,* of the thickness of two fingers, and afterwards wound very tight around the mast.

Two boys were fastened to both ends of this cord, of the age of seven or eight years, one of them holding in one hand a bow and in the other a bunch of arrows, the other boy carrying a hunting horn and a mirror. When the dance was completed the boys left the square; and the cord in unrolling raised them into the air,/134/ turning them around the mast, from which they kept retiring as the cord unwound, each serving as a counterpoise to the other. In the mean time the sixty dancers were executing a very regular step to the sound of six tambours, and to the voices of a dozen singers, the dancers observing the most complete silence. The music and dancing continued about half an hour. At the end of that time the boys began to descend. They took up as much time in reaching the ground as would suffice to repeat the Credo five or six times.

All the time they were in the air they continued moving their feet and arms, as if flying. As the cord is exactly measured, when it stops it is only a hand's breadth from the earth, so that they have only to lower their limbs to touch the ground, each alighting at about thirty paces distance from the mast on opposite sides. As soon as they have touched the earth the dancers and singers, uttering a loud cry, stop short, and the festival is finished.

The mast is allowed to remain eight or ten days; but when that time has expired a hundred or more Indians come and take it away. Detaching the idol from the summit, they carry it into the temple, where it remains until

130. Sic—*mitote* was Oviedo's spelling (N. *mitotl*, dance). A type of *areito* (n. 135), it included singing and dancing, masks, painted bodies, and featherwork. (O&V; León-Portilla, 57; Lehmann, 1012.)

131. Ageiteite had been rendered Agateyte by Oviedo, who also said he was called "the Old" (*agá, güe*, old). Oviedo visited him precisely on "a Thursday, for two days in January, 1528," and included the diagram of the plaza in which the event occurred. The long Oviedo extract here is from Book LXII, Chap. 11. (O&V; León-Portilla, 16, 51.)

132. Oviedo's pole is given as "80 palms"; as a modern unit the Spanish *palmo* suggests a height of about 50 feet. Squier's "48 hands" (today of 4 inches) would only be 16 feet. Squier's conversion cannot be explained. (Oviedo, iv 413-14.)

133. Both aloe (Aloe genus) and *pité* (sic—*pita*; e.g. piteira, the giant cabuya) furnish excellent fibers for cordage. *Cabuya*, here and in Squier's note below, is the common American agave or hemp sisal.

Cabuya, an American fibrous plant.

134. León-Portilla noted that *voladores*, "flyers," was a modern name for this performance, and that the Nicaraguan practice—introduced by the Nicaráos (see n. 23)—involved only two (boys) at a time, while in Mexico four (men) was common. Squier suggests here that the boys were attached to the cord on the ground and sent flying with a push to start the cord unwinding; Oviedo's own illustration shows they had to climb to the top of the pole and lower themselves into flight. Most historians refer to the event as a game, but the idol, bird-like costumes, and accoutrements had obvious religious meaning. (León-Portilla, 57, 76-78; Oviedo, iv 414; Healy, 345.)

the following anniversary, when the same scene is acted over again, which is certainly a spectacle well worth beholding. But nothing pleased me so much as their superb bunches of feathers, and the kind of clothing I have just described. Each couple, or quadrille, has a uniformity of color, and a different kind of cloth. The dancers were all handsome men and would have been so considered in Spain, or any other part of the world.

When this old cazique died and his son succeeded him—a very distinguished young man—I saw another kind of *areito*/135/ celebrated in the square of Tecoatega. It was Sunday, the 6th of May—Pentecost day. Twenty Indians painted black and red, and ornamented with bunches of feathers, were assembled under a sort of shed and were beating measure with their feet to the sound of six tambours. In the midst of the square, about twenty paces from the shed, were a dozen Indians disguised and painted red and black. They also had bunches of feathers on their heads, and carried javelins in their hands, and also hunting bows and balls of cotton. They danced in measure to the sound of this music.

About twelve paces to the right were four Indians, painted like the first. Upon their heads were perrukes or wigs, with long locks and bunches of feathers, as they wear them when they go to war. Three among them remained perfectly tranquil; the fourth danced alone, without removing himself more than a step or two from Tecoatega,/136/ who hurled sticks at him whenever he moved three or four paces off, hitting sometimes on the back, sometimes on the belly or thighs, taking care, however, not to hit him on the head. When the cazique hurled his stick at him he would bend his body, twisting or bending so as often to shun the blow; but not succeeding, he received the blows with a good grace, though they left marks behind them. When he had received ten or twelve blows another took his place; and so on, until the cazique had broken thirty whips on their bodies, the sticks being lighter than reeds and as large as a small finger. At the larger end was a ball of wax; but though the blows were not dangerous, it was a cruel sport, especially with people entirely naked.

When one of them received a blow he did not change his position, made no complaint, and far from having the air of one suffering, he prepared to receive another. The cazique would hurl the same stick at one three or four times, until he had broken it, or, having missed him, it had gone too far. He broke thirty sticks, as I have said before, upon the backs of those four dancers. The musicians, dancers, singers, and the beaten went away, uttering loud shouts and followed by a multitude of Indians, to visit the caziques of other villages. Four young Indians, whose skin had not as yet been broken, accompanied them to receive the blows; they took with them two Indians loaded with a kind of stick for that exercise.

When they were departed, I asked the cazique the reason for this ceremony; if it were a festival day among them, and what it might mean. He replied that it was not a festival, and that these Indians were from another village who were going to demand cacao from the cazique, and that these chiefs would serve them as he had; but that formerly the custom of striking their bodies with sticks was to see if they were brave, strong, and capable of bearing wounds and the fatigues of war. Certain it is, however, that the cazique, in hurling these sticks at them, did it with all his force, that he was young and vigorous, and that he gave them blows which caused the skin to rise up to the thickness of a finger.

The Indians have still other kinds of dances or *areitos*, accompanied with chants, which are very common, as I have before said in the course of this history, particularly at the death of caziques. These *areitos*, or songs, take the place of history, preserving the memory of past events, and celebrating the present.

Sometimes they are made use of to conceal treason, as happened at the time of the death of Christopher de Sotomayor,/137/ on the isle of St. John, as I have before mentioned in Book XVI, Chapter 5.

135. Also spelled *areyto*; Indian dance and song to celebrate victories, recite past deeds, conduct funerals, declare wars, and other solemn occasions. Below, Oviedo's text gives May 17, instead of the 6th. (Oviedo, iv 414; O&V.)

136. Squier neglects to introduce the son of Ageiteite, whose name Oviedo's printer set as "Fhecoatega" (for "Thecoatega," apparently the same typographical error as "Famagastad"—see n. 112). Squier uses the same spelling as the town (n. 97).

137. Sotomayor was a young Spanish nobleman who had an estate on Puerto Rico (Isle of St. John—sic—San Juan, the island's original name). When Indians there first realized the Spaniards were mortals, not gods, some caziques in 1511 conspired at an *areito* to fight them to the death. Warned of this, Sotomayor gathered a force to protect his property, but all were killed. The rebels were caught drunk and exhausted at another *areito*, a huge victory celebration. Wagenheim translated *areito* as "meeting," revealing why Oviedo holds the "dance" responsible for treachery. (Karl Wagenheim, Ed., *The Puerto Ricans: A Documentary History*. New York: Praeger, 1973, 23-25.)

They also celebrate *areitos* in which wine flows as abundantly as songs, until they fall to the ground dead drunk: those falling remaining so till their drunkenness has passed off, or till the next day; for those who are in this state are rather envied than blamed by their companions. It is not so much to dance as to drink, that they come together.

I will relate an incident of which I was a witness; and I vow, though a priest and some Spaniards were present on that occasion, I would have preferred to have been absent, for it was dangerous to find oneself in the presence of seventy or eighty idolatrous and brutal Indians, intoxicated, as well as their cazique, who could not love Christians—who as masters had rendered them slaves and who were endeavoring to destroy their rites and ceremonies. We could place no reliance on their friendship; we were far from all aid, from all succor, in the house of one of the most powerful caziques of the province, who could easily put us in a safe place in the sea, or on the land./138/

All these circumstances inspired us with much fear in the midst of that revel. It is true that this cazique, whose Indian name was Nicoya Nambi, was one of those who made the most show of friendship for Christians; he was baptized under the name D. Alonzo./139/ When Indians were needed and asked for, he always answered the call by saying, "I have no Indians, I have only Christians; and I will give them to you if you want them." And when we said, "Give us Christians to do such or such a thing," he would furnish as many as we wanted. Behold, then, what this cazique and his vassals did, though they had all been baptized Saturday, August 19th, 1526.

Don Alonzo, Cazique of Nicoya, whose name was Nambi, which signifies "dog" in the Chorotegan language, coming upon the village square about two hours before night, eighty or one hundred Indians assembled in a corner of this square and began to celebrate their *areito*, singing and dancing. They must have been common people; for in he went in ceremony to seat himself in another corner of the square, upon a kind of long seat. The principal officers and sixty or eighty other Indians took their places about him, and a young girl brought them drink in small calabashes of the size of a glass—a kind of wine, very strong and a little acid, that they make of maize and call *chicha*./140/ This drink resembles chicken soup in its color, mixed with one or two yolks of eggs.

As soon as they began to drink, the cazique took a packet of tobacco leaves, about six inches in length and of a finger's thickness, made of a kind of leaf rolled and fastened with thread. They cultivate this plant with the greatest care, and they make rolls of it, which they kindle at one end and which burns slowly during an entire day. They place the other end in their mouth, inhaling the smoke from time to time, and after a little while emitting it through the mouth and nostrils. Each Indian had one of these rolls of leaves called *yupoquete*/141/ in their language, and *tobacco* in the island of Haiti.

138. A closer reading might be "... where—at sea or on land—they were disposed to fly off any way they wished." (Oviedo, iv 416.)

139. "D." (don), the Spanish title for a gentleman, was often bestowed on Indian chiefs to signify recognition of élite status among their people. Alonzo has been introduced earlier (see n. 37), and his name twice listed in the glossaries.

140. Alcoholic drink made from fermented maize. In his book Squier also described a modern native alcoholic drink, *chiche*, made from the juice of coyol palm. (Squier, ii 155.)

141. A translation of this paragraph used by Healy is more literal:

And as soon as they had begun to drink, the *cacique* himself brought forward a handful of rolls of tobacco, each as long as the distance from the end of one's thumb to the tip of one's forefinger, and consisting of a certain leaf rolled up and tied with two or three thin cords of agave fiber, which leaf and the plant to which it pertains, they cultivate with great diligence, in order to obtain these tobaccos; and they lighted a small space at one end, and it consumes itself (like a *pibete*) until it is all burned away, which process lasts during a day; and from time to time they placed it in their mouths, at the end opposite to that which was burning, and they suck in its smoke for a short while, and then remove it, keeping their mouths closed, and holding the breath for a time, after which they breathe, and this smoke emerges through their mouths and noses.

Pibete is not defined. *Yupoquete* (Oviedo's *ya-poquete*) or *puquiet* primarily meant a cigar; Stone considered it a Chorotegan invention.

In the Petén (1695) "cigar" described tobacco (*Nicotiana tabacum*—a strong wild form) wrapped in the leaf of the nance tree (*Birsonima crassifolia*). This was coated with clay and painted in decorative colors. It was made by Lacandons in large quantities and used in trade. The clay coating confused some early historians into thinking a fired ceramic was involved, but Robicsek observed that in Central America the true pipe was known only in Nicaragua and

Servants of both sexes brought them alternately calabashes filled with this drink and with that prepared from cacao. They drank continually three or four swallows of this last, and passed it from hand to hand. During all this time they did not cease from inhaling this smoke and playing the tambour and beating their hands in measure, while the others sang. They kept together till midnight, and the greater part lay on the ground dead drunk. But as the symptoms of drunkenness vary among all men, some appeared dead and made no movement; others wept or cried; some made extravagant leaps.

When they were in this state their wives and children came to look for them and take them home with them: some continued asleep till the next-day noon; others till night, according as they had drunk more or less. Those who had not drunk so much were despised by the others and regarded as bad warriors. It was truly frightful to hear them weep and cry, and still more to see them drink in that manner; for the less we knew of the manner in which the festival was to finish, the greater the danger appeared to be. The females of higher rank have similar revels among themselves.

We feared more than once that the five or six Spaniards present would be victims of this debauch; for this reason we kept ourselves on our guard and our arms in our hands. For, though not numerous enough to defend ourselves against so many enemies, we were determined to sell our lives dearly, and to kill the cazique and principal chiefs, deprived of whom the others are nothing; for these Indians disband generally when they have lost their leaders.

They had still another kind of *areito*, which is celebrated in the following manner, three times a year, on certain prescribed days. They regard it as their major festival. The Cazique of Nicoya, his principal chiefs, and the greater part of his vassals of both sexes painted their bodies and assumed their most beautiful bunches of feathers. They executed a circular dance, in which the women took hold of each other's hands or arms; the men formed a circle around them, taking hold of each other in the same manner. They left a space of about four or five paces in which, as in that between the females, were placed Indians who gave drink to the dancers, who kept on drinking and dancing; the men making with head and body a multitude of movements which the women imitated.

The women all had on this day a pair of *cutaras*,/142/ or new shoes. They danced in this way for four or more hours in the main square of the village, in front of the temple, and around the elevation which is used for sacrifices. Afterwards they took a man and a woman appointed for that purpose, made them to mount this mound, cut into their breasts and tore out their hearts, and offered to the gods the first blood that flowed; then they cut off their heads and also the heads of four or five others upon the large stone at the top of the mound. They offered the blood of the other victims to their particular gods, and stained their idols with it; they also sprinkled their priests and sacrificers, or—to express their calling better—their infernal butchers. Afterwards the dead bodies were thrown from the top to the bottom of the mound, where the Indians collected them in order to eat them, as a sacred and excellent nourishment.

At the moment the sacrifice is finished, it is usual for the women to utter a loud cry and fly to the woods and mountains, each by herself or two by two. They go in spite of the will of their parents and husbands, who strive to bring them back by prayers, promises, or presents. As to those who need more severe means, blows with sticks are made use of; then they are confined till their drunkenness has passed away. The woman who is caught the furthest off is praised and esteemed above the others.

On the same or the next day after these festivals, a number of sheaves of maize are brought and laid around the mound of sacrifices. All then, without any exception, beginning with the priest of Satan and the cazique, draw near, and, cutting the tongue or the private parts, each according to his devotion, with very large stones,

Costa Rica. (Some specimens with two stems suggest they were for snuffing rather than smoking; Oviedo similarly describes *tabaco* as a Y-shaped instrument whose two upper tubes were placed in the nostrils for inhaling.)

Robicsek credited Oviedo as first European to report (elsewhere) the analgesic property of tobacco smoking, useful in treating syphilis. Among the Aztecs tobacco also played an important part in rites and ceremonies; the Nahuatl word for tobacco, *picietl*, is undoubtedly a cognate of *puquiet*. For a 1695 Lacandón ceremony involving cigar smoking, see Fray Antonio Marjil de Jesus, Fray Lazaro de Mazariegos, Fray Blas Guillen, *A Spanish Manuscript Letter on the Lacandones, in the Archives of the Indies at Seville.* Culver City: Labyrinthos, 1984.

(Francis Robicsek, *The Smoking Gods: Tobacco in Maya Art, History, and Religion.* Norman: University of Oklahoma Press, 1978, 4, 9, 13, 20, 29-30, 37-38, 58; O&V; Lehmann, 1016; Oviedo, iv 416; Stone, 221.)

142. See n. 104.

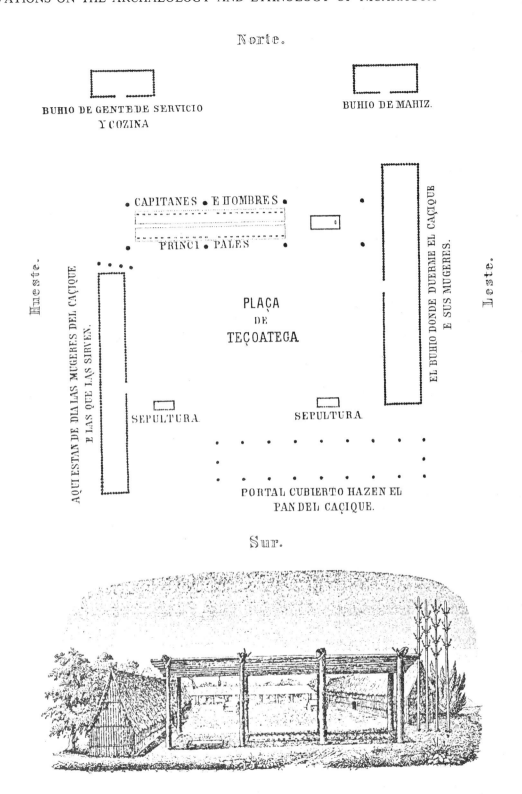

"Plaça de Teçoatega," plan and elevation based on Oviedo's own artwork which, with the labels "right" and "left" (which did not mean "east" and "west") caused Squier some confusion. The draftsman has substituted compass directions. Since this plaza had no temple or altar, Radell has suggested it was Ageiteite's private area, not the main plaza. Tecoatega today is a town called El Viejo. (Radell, 40-43.)

they let the blood fall on this maize, then dividing it in such a manner that each one may receive a little. They eat it as though it were a blessed thing.

Among the various athletic games to which these Indians were addicted was one which might be called the revolving game. A long bar was fixed horizontally on the top of a post, so as to turn or revolve readily. At each end were fastened pegs by which the performers could hold on. They then took hold of these, and running rapidly set the bar revolving; after which, throwing themselves horizontally in the air, by an adroit balancing or see-saw movement they made the bar revolve with the rapidity, says Oviedo, "of a knife-grinder's wheel."

CALENDAR

The fact that there were at least two distinct stocks or nations in Nicaragua, which are described collectively by the chroniclers, has led to some degree of confusion in giving satisfactory information upon points like that, for instance, of their calendars. It appears, however, that all or nearly all the information which Bobadilla and others obtained in relation to these calendars was procured from the Niquirans, or descendants of Mexicans.

DAYS OF THE MONTH AND THEIR ORDER.

True Order.	Order acc. to Oviedo.	Nicaragua.	Signs.	Mexico.	Significance.
1	9	Cipat,		Cipactli,	Sea animal.
2	10	Hecat,		Ehecatl,	Wind or air.
3	11	Cali,		CALLI,	House.
4	12	Quespal,		Cuetzpalin,	Lizard.
5	13	Coat,		Cohuatl,	Serpent.
6	14	Migiste,		Miquiztli,	Death.
7	15	Mazat,		Mazatl,	Deer.
8	16	Toste,		TOCHTLI,	Rabbit.
9	17	At,		Atl,	Water.

True Order.	Order acd. to Oviedo.	Nicaragua.	Signs.	Mexico.	Significance.
10	18	Izquindi,		Itzcuintli,	Dog.
11	19	Ocomate,		Ozomatli,	Ape.
12	20	Malinal,		Malinalli,	Grass.
13	1	Acato,		ACATL,	Reed.
14	2	Ocelot,		Ocelotl,	Tiger.
15	3	Oate,		Quauhtli,	Eagle.
16	4	Cozgaconte,		Cozcaquauhtli,	Bird.
17	5	Olin,		Ollin,	Movements of Sun.
18	6	Topecat,		TECPATL,	Flint.
19	7	Quiauvit,		Quiahuitl,	Rain.
20	8	Sochit,		Xochtli,	Flower.

He inquired of them the number of their festivals; but either those festivals bore the names of the days of the month, or the Indians misunderstood the question; for they gave him the names of the twenty days of the month, which are the same as those of the Mexican calendar. The table above shows the names of the days as given to Bobadilla, and the order in which he presents them, as also their true order, their names in Mexico, and the signs by which they were distinguished.

The vigintesimal/143/ numeration of the nations of the Mexican stock, it will be observed, was applied to the division of time. And as five (a hand), ten (both hands), and fifteen (hands and one foot) in the Mexican numeration had uncompounded names, so the twenty days of the month were divided into four periods of five days each. This seems to be the rational mode of accounting for this division of time; for the period of twenty days has no relation to natural phenomena, such for instance as the periods of the moon.

The Mexican civil year consisted of eighteen periods or months, of twenty days, with five supplementary days, *nemontemi*,/144/ or dead days, thus making 365 days. The deficiency which we supply by the intercalation of one day every fourth or leap year they supplied by the intercalation of thirteen days at the close of every cycle of 52 years.

But besides this the Mexicans had a period, or sacred year, of 260 days, consisting of thirteen periods of twenty days. All the feasts, religious rites, and nativities were adjusted in reference to this period, which has hence been called the sacred year. The days of this period were distinguished by the signs of the days, and a series of dots equivalent to numerals, from one to thirteen.

It is obvious that by this combination no two days during this period could have both the same name and the same numerical character.

But this combination would not answer for the entire period of 360 days, for the days of the fourteenth month would have the same sign and number with those of the first. In order to obviate this, a third series of signs was introduced, nine in number, and called Lords of the Night./145/ They were as follows:

Names	Significance	Names	Significance
Xiuhtecutli	Lord of the Year; Fire	Atl	Water, or the Goddess of Water
Tecpatl	Flint	Tlazolteotl	Goddess of Love
Xochitl	Flower	Tepogolotl	Mountain Goddess
Cinteotl	Goddess of Maize	Quiahuitl	Rain; the God Tlaloc
Miquiztli	Death		

It will at once be understood that as nine is not a factor of 260, no two days in the entire 360 could have the same numbers; consequently the combination could accurately distinguish any one from the others.

No doubt the same system existed in Nicaragua among the descendants of the Mexicans there. It is true Bobadilla reports that each month was called *cemponalli*/146/ (which is the Mexican term for twenty), and that the year contained *ten* of these, or 200 days; but this is no doubt a mistake of the chronicler.

Among the Mexicans, as I have said, a series of 52 years made up a cycle, called Xiuhmopilli,/147/ which signified "the tying up of years," and was indicated by a sign representing a bundle of reeds. This cycle was divided into four periods of thirteen each, i.e. thirteen numerals and four signs./148/ The signs were:

143. See n. 48.

144. The five remaining days of the year (after 360) were considered unlucky, nameless, and worthless; they had no symbols or numbers. The *nemontemi* ("days left over and profitless") fell in February. (Vaillant, 193; Durán, 395, 469.)

145. Squier's list is a mixture of gods' names (items 1, 4, 7, 8) and attributes (item 2 for the god Itzli; 3, for Tonatiuh; 5, for Mictlantecutli; 6, for Chalchiuhtecutli; 9, for Tlaloc. These gods governed the 9 hours of the night as astrological omens; they did not really augment the calendar. (Vaillant, 190; Soustelle, 111, 113.)

146. *Cemponalli*, Oviedo's *cempoualli* (N., "twenty"), was the word for the twenty-day "month"; the eighteen months of course would have their own individual names. (Lehmann, 1010; Vaillant, 186; O&V.)

147. *Xiuhmopilli* (N. "Tying up of the years") represented a 52-year Aztec "century," at the beginning of which household and temple furnishings were destroyed and new ones made. Vaillant has noted that such ritually broken pottery makes dating fairly exact for archaeological purposes. (Vaillant, 68, 91, 194.)

148. The significance is that the four 13-year periods always began with one of these four days. The "names" are superimposed over the solar year sign, *xiuitl*. Note that the *calli* (house) outline here is right side up, whereas it is horizontal in the table on p. 42.

SIGNS. NAMES.

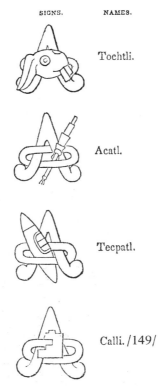

Tochtli.

Acatl.

Tecpatl.

Calli. /149/

149. Squier ends his ethnological report here, somewhat abruptly. In his history of Nicaragua, however, he devoted a few more pages to Bobadilla and his continued efforts to convert the natives. These were indeed not ethnological matters, but they illustrate the enormous problems the clergy would face:

The Fray Bobadilla was piously indignant at the practices of the Indians, and longed to be able to prove to them how insignificant their *teotes* were as compared with the God and his subordinates whom he worshiped. In this respect he was favored, for there were several manifestations from above in his behalf, hardly less extraordinary than those which befell the Spaniards in Mexico. . . . Thus, there had been no rain in Nicaragua for a long time; but upon the Fray's arrival at the Indian towns it rained for five consecutive days, which he regarded as a miracle, and straightaway assured the Indians if they would become Christians, "it would rain whenever it was wanted. . . ." The Indians approved of the rain, and in order to secure it, allowed the Fray to collect "a large number of idols, heads of deer, and parcels stained with blood, in the public square, and give them to the flames." They even allowed him to convert their temple into a Christian church, which he did by sprinkling it with holy water, and setting up within it a cross and an image of the Virgin, which last he especially enjoined them to keep clean. . . .

But the miracle of the five days' steady rain was nothing compared with what happened to the Fray in the province of Matearas, where he found a child dying, to which he administered the rite of baptism, whereupon the babe ejaculated "*cruz!*" and died! This so astonished the mother that she exclaimed that she saw her child ascending to heaven. The child had a magnificent funeral in consequence, and the Fray made the most of the miracle, inducing not less than ten thousand Indians to be baptized on the strength of it. . . .

But the chronicler [Oviedo] did not put much faith in these conversions. . . . In his opinion these baptisms did no good, and were only valuable to swell reports to be sent to Spain. "Far better," he sensibly ejaculates, "is it to instruct and truly Christianize one Indian, than to baptize thousands who know not what it is to be a Christian, or what to do to be saved. I should like to ask those," he continues, "who have been god-fathers to four and five hundred Indians, what they have done for their god-children?" . . .

(Squier, ii 360-62.)

IDOL FROM MOMOTOMBITA. NO I.

BIBLIOGRAPHY

Abel-Vidor, Suzanne, "Gonzalo Fernandez de Oviedo y Valdes: His Work and His Nicaragua, 1527-1529." *Costa Rican Art and Archaeology: Essays in Honor of Frederick R. Mayer*, Frederick W. Lange, Ed. Boulder: University of Colorado Museum, 1988, 263-89.

Bancroft, Hubert H., *History of Central America*, 3 Vols. San Francisco: Bancroft, 1882.

Bernal, Ignacio, *A History of Mexican Archaeology: The Vanished Civilizations of Middle America*. London: Thames & Hudson, 1980.

Chapman, Anne M., *Los Nicarao y Los Chorotega según las Fuentes Historicas*. San José: Universidad de Costa Rica, 1960.

Creamer, Winifried, and Jonathan Haas, "Tribe versus Chiefdom in Lower Central America." *American Antiquity*, Vol. 50 (1985), 738-54.

Davies, Nigel, *The Toltecs: Until the Fall of Tula*. Norman: University of Oklahoma Press, 1977.

Deuel, Leo, *Conquistadors without Swords: Archaeologists in the Americas*. New York: St. Martin's Press, 1967.

Durán, Fray Diego, *Book of the Gods and Rites* and *The Ancient Calendar*, Fernando Horcasitas and Doris Heyden, Trans., Eds. Norman: University of Oklahoma Press, 1971.

Friedrichsthal, Emanuel, "Notes on the Lake of Nicaragua and the Province of Chontales, in Guatemala //sic//." Royal Geographical Society (London), *Journal*, Vol. 11 (1841), 97-100.

Handbook of Middle American Indians //HMAI//, Robert Wauchope, Gen. Ed. Vol. IV. *Archaeological Frontiers and External Connections*, Gordon F. Eckholm and Gordon R. Willey, Eds.; Vol. XIII, *Guide to Ethnohistorical Sources*, Part 2, Howard F. Cline, Ed., 1973. Austin: University of Texas Press.

Hay, Clarence L., et al., *The Maya and Their Neighbors: Essays on Middle American Anthropology and Archaeology*. New York: 1940/Dover 1977.

Healy, Paul F., *Archaeology of the Rivas Region, Nicaragua*. Waterloo, Ontario: Laurier University Press, 1980.

Keen, Benjamin, *The Aztec Image in Western Thought*. New Brunswick: Rutgers University Press, 1971.

Kidder, Alfred, II, "South American Penetrations." Hay et al., 441-59.

Landa, Fray Diego de, *Landa's Relación de las Cosas de Yucatan: A Translation //1566//*, Alfred M. Tozzer, Ed. Cambridge: Peabody Museum, Papers, Vol. 18 (1941).

Las Casas, Fray Bartolomé, *Apologética historia de las Indias. . . .*, Serrano y Sanz, Ed. Madrid: 1909.

Latham, Robert G., *The Natural History of the Varieties of Man*. London: van Voorst, 1850.

—, *Man and His Migrations*. London: van Voorst, 1851.

Lehmann, Walter, *Zentral-Amerika*, 2 Vols. Berlin: Dietrich Reimer, 1920.

León-Portilla, Miguel, "Religión de los Nicaraos: Análisis y Comparación de Tradiciones Culturales Nahuas." *Estudios de Cultura Nahuatl*, Vol. 10 (1972), 11-112.

Lothrop, Samuel K., "The Southeastern Frontier of the Maya." *American Anthropologist*, Vol. 41 (1939), 42-54.

—, "South America as Seen from Middle America." Hay et al., 417-29.

—, "Archaeology of Lower Central America." HMAI, Vol. IV, 180-208.

Mason, J. Alden, "The Native Languages of Middle America." Hay et al., 52-87.

Molina, Fray Alonso de, *Vocabulario en lengua castellana y Mexicana y Mexicana y castellana //1571//*, 2nd Ed., Miguel León-Portilla, Ed. Mexico City: Porrúa, 1977.

Oviedo y Valdes, Capt. Gonzalo Fernandez de, *Historia general y natural de las indias, islas y tierra-firme del mar oceano //O&V//*, 14 Vols. Asuncion, Paraguay: Guarania, 1945. (Useful glossary at end of Vol. 14.)

—, //Oviedo//, 5 Vols., Juan Perez de Tudela Bueso, Ed. Madrid: Atlas, 1959. (All citations are to this work.)

Padden, R. C., *The Hummingbird and the Hawk: Conquest and Sovereignty in the Valley of Mexico, 1503-1541*. New York: Harper, 1967.

Palacio, Diego Garcia de, *Letter to the King of Spain //1576//*, Ephraim G. Squier, Trans. Culver City: Labyrinthos, 1985.

Radell, David R., "Historical Geography of Western Nicaragua: The Spheres of Influence of Leon, Granada, and Managua, 1519-1965." Manuscript, 1969.

Sauer, Carl O., *The Early Spanish Main*. Berkeley: University of California Press, 1969.

Soustelle, Jacques, *Daily Life of the Aztecs on the Eve of the Spanish Conquest*, Patrick O'Brian, Trans. Stanford: Stanford University Press, 1961.

Spinden, Herbert J., "The Chorotegan Culture Area." International Congress of Americanists, *Proceedings*, 1924-1925, 529-45.

Squier, Ephraim G., *Nicaragua: Its People, Scenery, Monuments, and the Proposed Interocean Canal*, 2 Vols. New York: Harper, 1852. (All citations are to this work.)

—, "Observations on the Archaeology and Ethnology of Nicaragua." American Ethnological Society (New York), *Transactions*, Vol. 3 (1853), 83-158.

—, *The States of Central America: Their Geography, Topography, Climate, Population, Resources, Productions, Commerce, Political Organizations, Aborigines, etc., etc.* New York: Harper, 1858.

—, *Nicaragua: Its People, Scenery, Monuments, Resources, Condition, and Proposed Canal . . .: A Revised Edition.* New York: Harper, 1860. (One volume.)

Stansifer, Charles L., "The Central American Career of E. George Squier." New Orleans: Tulane University, Ph.D. Dissertation (1959).

Stone, Doris, "Synthesis of Lower Central American Ethnohistory." HMAI, Vol. IV, 209-33.

Strong, William D., "Anthropological Problems in Central America." Hay et al., 377-85.

Tedlock, Dennis, Trans., *Popol Vuh: The Definitive Edition of the Mayan Book of the Dawn of Life and the Glories of Gods and Kings.* New York: Simon & Schuster, 1985.

Ternaux-Compans, Henri, *Recueil de documents et mémoires originaux sur l'histoire des possessions spagnoles dans l'Amerique*, 20 Vols. Paris: 1840.

Vaillant, George C., *The Aztecs of Mexico: Origin, Rise and Fall of the Aztec Nation.* Harmondsworth, Middlesex: Penguin Books, 1950.

Wolf, Eric R., *Sons of the Shaking Earth.* Chicago: University of Chicago Press, 1959.

INDEX

Nicaraguas (tribe), 17
Nicaráo (chief), 6, 21
Nicaráo (tribe), 18;
    see also Niquirans
Nicoya, gulf, 6, 7, 12, 18, 21
Nicoya, land of Niquirans, 27, 39
Nicoya Nambi (chief), 39
Nicoyans (tribe), see Niquirans
Nindiri, Tenderi (site), 21
Niquirans (tribe), 6, 31, 37, 40
    Aztec gods of, 28
    calendar of, 42-43
    classified, 8
    vocabulary of, 8
North America, Indians of, 14
Numeration, Indian, 15

Oate, quauhtli (day), 43
Oaxaca (Mexico), 8, 17
Obsidian, blades of, 27
Ocelot, ocelotl (day), 43
Oçomate, ozomatli (day), 43
Olin, ollin (day), 43
Olmecs (Mexico), 31
    enslave Indians, 17
Omecíhuatl, Omeyatecígoat (godess), 31
Ometecuhtli, Omeyateite (god), 31
Ometepe, Ometepec, island, 6, 9, 20
    vocabulary from, 9
Order of Mercy, see Mercedarians
Oregon, Indians of, 19
Original Voyages and Relations concerning America (Ternaux-Compans), 22
Orota, Oroti, Orosi (volcano), 8, 21
Orotiña, gulf, see Nicoya
Orotiña (language), 7
Orotiñans (tribe), 7
    vocabulary from, 8
Otomanguean (language), 6
Oviedo y Valdez, Gonzales Hernández de, 21, 28
    on Indians, 6, 7, 24-25, 26, 37
    on Indian products, 3, 25, 27, 40
    on languages, 6, 8, 27
    on natural products, 7, 24, 40
    on Nicaragua, 7, 12, 21, 25
Oxomoco (god), 29

Pacific Ocean, 17
    shellfish from, 2
Pacific coast, Indians on, 5-6
Palacio, Diego Garcia de, 25
Palenque, 16
Palestine, 18
Palm, for mats, 2
Panama, 4, 6, 12, 21, 26, 28
Parents, Indians as, 24
Paya (tribe), see Poya
Pearls, as ornamentation, 27
Pedrarias Dávila, see Arias de Avila

Peonage, 4
Peru, 4, 5, 28, 36
    Indians of, 15, 18, 25
    language similarities, 8-9
Petate (mat), made by Indians, 2
    of cazique, 25
Peten (Guatemala), 16
    cigar in, 39
Physique, of Nicaraguan Indians, 25
Pilzintecuhtli (god), 28
Pipe, smoking, 39-40
Pipil (tribe), 31
    in San Salvador, 18
Piskwaus (tribe), 19
Pita, pité, cord made from, 26, 37
Plain of León, see León
Plaza, 25; Oviedo on, 37, 41
Poconchí (language), 8, 16
Pokomam (language), 8
Pole, for idol, 37
Popol Vuh, 29, 36
Posultega, Posuetega, Poçoltega, 16
Pottery, Indians make, 2-3; at Rivas, 6
Poyas (tribe), 5, 6
Present condition of Indians, 1-5
Primitive condition of Nicaragua, 21-22
Property, Indian, 24-25
Prostitution, 24
Pueblo, defined, 3
Pueblo Indians, 14
Puerto Rico, areito in, 38
Puquiet, see Yupoquete
Purple (dye), 2

Quetzalcoatl, 28, 35
Quezaltenango (Guatemala), 19
Quiahtéotl, rain god, 31-32
Quiahuitl, rain, 44
Quiatéot (god), 31
Quiauvit, quiahuitl (day), 43
Quiché (tribe), 8, 19, 29
    language, 8, 16
Quichoid languages, 8
Quiriguá (Guatemala), 19

Rabbit, 17
Ramas (tribe), 5, 6
Rape, 24
Reception house, of cazique, 25
Relación of Mérida, 3
Relationship, degree of, 24
Religion, Indian, 7, 28-36
    similarities, 20
Resin, burned at marriage, 24
Revolving game, 42
Right to live, Indian, 4
Río Mico, 9
Rivas, isthmus, 6
Robbery, punished, 25
Robicsek, Francis, 39-40

Rosary, worn, 3
Roys, Ralph L., 26
Rubber people, 17, 31
Rula, house dog, 24

Sacred year (260 days), 44
Sacrifice, human, 6, 17, 18, 33, 36
    at *areito*, 40
    prisoners for, 23
    at volcano, 7
Sahagún, Fray Bernardino de, 18, 29
Salish (tribe), 19
Salt Lake Valley, 18
Salteba, Xalteba, (place), 7
San Salvador, Indians, 16, 21
    Mexican colony at, 18
San Juan River, 5
Sandals (*cutares*), 3, 26
Santa Catarina Mita (Guatemala), 17
Santa Cruz del Quiché, 19
Sauer, Carl O., 26, 27
Scalp, 24; see also Head
Seat (*petate*), of official, 25
Seville (Spain), 1
Shield, for combat, 27
Shoe-shaped vessel, 20
Shoes, 3; see also Sandals
Sinca, Lenca, Xincan (language), 16
Singers, at *mitole*, 37
Sisal, 37
Skirt, woman's, 3
Skitsuish (tribe), 19
Skull, as trophy, 36
Slavery, 24, 25
    Arias de Avila and, 4
    captives sacrificed, 33
    Indians allow, 17, 25
    trade in Nicaragua, 4
Smithsonian Institution, 20
Snuffing, tobacco, 40
Sochit, xochitli (day), 43
Social organization, Indian, 22-27
Soconusco, Indians subjugated by Olmecs in, 7
Sodomy, 24
Sotomayor, Christopher de, 38
Soustelle, Jacques, 24, 28
South America, Indians of, 6
    inventions of, 9
Spain, policy in America, 1
Spinden, Herbert J., 6
Spindle, for cotton spinning, 1-2
Spinning wheel, cotton, 1
St. John (Juan, Puerto Rico), 38
St. Laurence Valley, 14
Stansifer, Charles, 20
Stephens, John L., 19
Stone, Doris, 6, 36, 39
Strong, William D., 5
Subtiaba (place), 21